S0-ASL-845

THE
BRAND
GLOSSARY

Edited by Jeff Swystun

Interbrand   palgrave
macmillan

Introduction

The most powerful ideas are simple, and brands adhere to the same rules. Just ask a few people you know, who aren't in the industry, and you will find that they are able to articulate the idea behind a great brand in just a few short, focused words. Good branding is therefore "easier said than done."

Creating simple, but powerful, differentiation in the minds of your customers, your staff, indeed all your stakeholders, requires a clear and compelling vision that is expressed in everything you do; from product to service, through environments, to the people you hire, and the way you talk about yourself. Maintaining such simplicity throughout the complex systems, processes, and politics that characterize modern business is a considerable task, requiring absolute focus, passion, and conviction. No wonder then, that as competition increases, brands are playing an ever-increasing role in business strategy.

It is now common knowledge that branding is fundamental to business success, and probably why our *Best Global Brands* league table is one of the top three published business rankings in the world. At Interbrand we have always placed great emphasis on the need for a balance between the logical and the creative. Brands, after all, live in our heads and our hearts.

But ultimately, brands are value generators for business and this is our true obsession; using our creativity and strategic thinking to create value. Indeed, increasingly we are serving the need for a deeper understanding of how brands generate value and the use of that information to inform better business decisions.

Initially, we thought it strange to be creating a glossary, which by its nature makes complexity easy to understand, about a subject area that demands simplicity! But the language of branding simply reflects the depth of the subject and, as we all know, brand language is varied, misunderstood, and often abused. This book became our duty, indeed a labour of love!

With this glossary, the people of Interbrand have set out to demystify, educate, inform, and entertain. We hope to provide a common language allowing us, the brand practitioners, owners, and otherwise interested parties, to focus our debate and energy on improving our use and understanding of brands as a force for business.

A simple idea indeed.

Jez Frampton
Group Chief Executive
Interbrand

I D E A

Behind every great brand is a great idea

Acknowledgements

If you are setting out to edit a glossary (and I am quite confident that few of you are) there are three lessons worth sharing. The first is to more than double your original estimate of the time required to complete such an effort. I affectionately compare the process to that of cutting off a head of the mythical monster Hydra – complete one term and it produces two more.

The second lesson is to ensure it is not the only project you are pursuing. Diversions will maintain your sanity and actually offer greater context. Through the process I found myself re-examining many areas that are taken for granted, such as, how we process communications and information, how we purchase brands, and how subjectivity and objectivity compete in decision-making. This helped shape the content.

The third and most important lesson is to have access to the leading subject matter experts. I thankfully had access to over 1,100 of my colleagues, representing different branding disciplines from all regions of the world. Their brainpower is truly impressive and I wish to acknowledge outstanding individual contributions.

Jason Baer (New York) provided expertise in naming and verbal identity with his infectious enthusiasm for this aspect of branding. Walter Brecht (Cologne) put himself in the place of his clients to continually challenge the content. Jean-Baptiste Danet (Paris) provided calm guidance and support during the entire process. Rita Clifton (London), a recognized expert on global branding, offered valuable feedback throughout. Julie Cottineau (New York), innovator of Brand Tango, lent a hand in various areas. Matthew Cross (San Francisco) ensured we covered all the terms important to his clients and students.

Alfredo Fraile (Madrid) provided a distinct and valuable European perspective. Jan Lindemann (London), a leader in brand valuation and measurement, made sure we kept matters appropriately tangible. Jessica Lyons (Melbourne) lent a hand from down under. Q Malandrino (New York) shared his expertise in brand culture. Jerome McDonnell (New York) focused on brand protection. Andy Milligan (London), author of many brand books, identified current trends. Lorena Noriega (Buenos Aires), who has a great passion for brand consulting, undertook tremendous research.

Larry Oakner (New York) articulated the differences between internal communications and brand culture. Terry Oliver (Tokyo) made sure that the book took into account the rapid changes taking place in Asia. Sam Osborn (Melbourne) was a tremendous support in content, comment, and editing. Sarng Park (Seoul) represented the views of brand-savvy South Korea. Re Perez (New York) provided guidance in the area of brand culture. Román Pérez-Miranda (New York) offered up the Latin America-Iberia perspective, a region whose brand sophistication is growing exponentially.

Robin Rusch (New York), the first editor of leading brand website brandchannel.com, contributed to the online branding and brand automation areas. Gary Singer (New York) was a great supporter and contributor to key terms. Bev Tudhope (Toronto) helped on the nexus of branding and investor communications. Thomas Zara (New York) took on terms with vigor and intellect.

Decoding the mystery of consultant speak

Branding has a huge creative and visual component and this is reflected in the theme and design of this glossary. Chris Campbell led the creative direction of the book with support from Gary Ludwig. Lynne Northwood developed the original concept. John Spicer ensured that the dual efforts of content and design wove seamlessly together. Ronan Tiongson and Michèle Champagne designed the majority of the illustrations and overall layout that help immeasurably to bring the terms to life.

Stephen Rutt of Palgrave-Macmillan deserves thanks for his great support and even greater patience. Thanks to Steven Schwartz, a thirty-year veteran of written business communications, who worked on the terms and ensured quality and consistency. A very special thanks to Lisa Marsala, who worked tirelessly to see this book to market from initial concept, to term development, to design, to marketing and promotion.

What you will find within is a great start, but it is admittedly a work-in-progress. A dictionary can claim to be definitive while a glossary, though a respected authority, captures a point in time in the evolution of a certain practice. We expect the glossary will require frequent updates to stay apace with branding's development. We also anticipate and welcome feedback in the hope of establishing a shared lexicon from which all can benefit. Send your comments through www.interbrand.com and visit www.brandchannel.com to contribute to the brand debate.

From the outset, we intended the glossary to be a valuable companion rather than a dusty reference book forgotten on a shelf. It contains terms, illustrations big and small, facts, and relevant quotes, all to help communicate the practice of branding. The book is designed to inspire you to learn, question, and explore. I will know we have been successful when I see someone with their dog-eared copy full of Post-its, marked pages, doodles, and scribbled ideas for the next great brand.

Jeffrey Swystun
Global Director
Interbrand

A valuable brand companion

"A brand is a living entity –
and it is enriched or
undermined cumulatively
over time, the product of a
thousand small gestures."

Michael Eisner

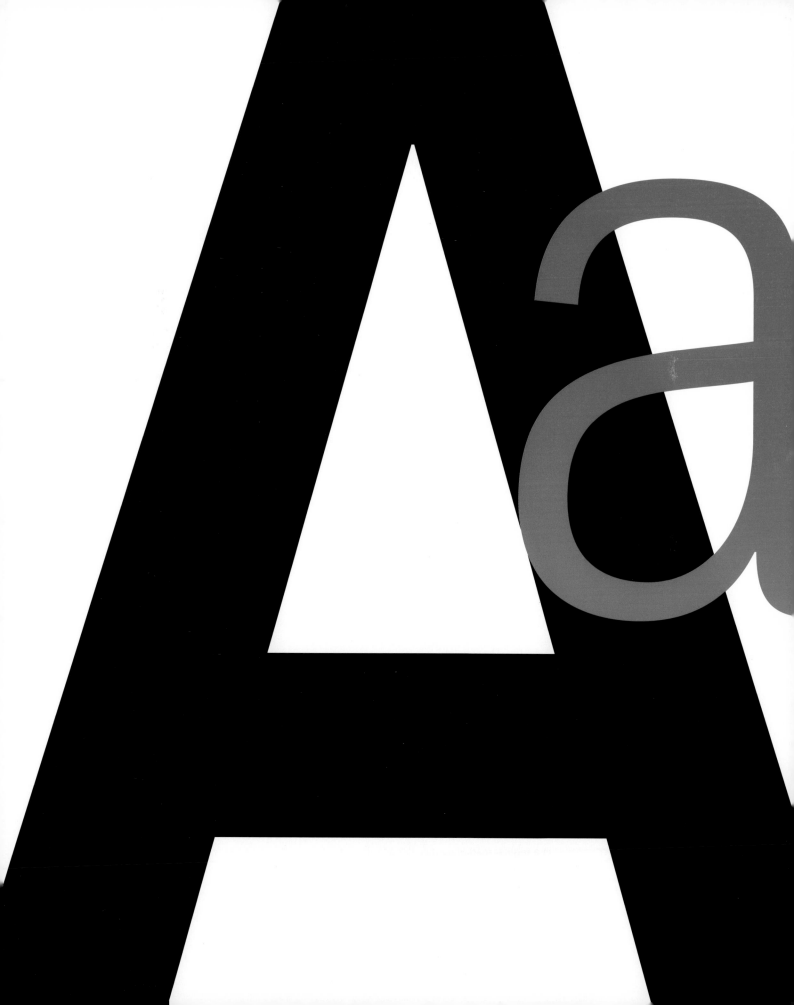

Above-the-line Communications

This term refers to marketing communications involving the purchase of traditional media such as television, radio, print, and outdoors; media in which results can be measured. As marketing and communications options have expanded, and advertising agency compensation has moved from commission-based to fee-based, this term has become increasingly dated and now reflects what traditional advertising agencies included in their base commission rate rather than what impact the media would have had on customers.

Account Executive

In advertising agencies, this term refers to a person who is the day-to-day contact between the agency and the client. Over the years, the account executive function has evolved to exert a more strategic influence in managing agency relationships. Newer titles such as *account planner* and *relationship manager* are used interchangeably with account executive. Similar terms are used in branding and design consultancies. The fact remains that one individual from the agency or consulting organization must assume responsibility for the satisfaction of the client.

Ad Hoc Research

This is a one-off type of research carried out at a specific time for a specific client. Ad hoc research differs from longer term, ongoing studies such as sales and profitability monitoring, satisfaction tracking, and perception rankings.

Adapted Marketing Mix

This is a combination of product offerings first marketed in one geography that is then altered to suit local conditions in additional markets. As in a regular marketing mix, the adaptive mix comprises the Four P's of product, price, promotion, and place. Also known as *distribution*, that is, having the product available for purchase in the target market.

Product   Price   Promotion   Place

Added-value

The tangible or intangible benefit provided by a product or service that generally commands a higher price and engenders customer loyalty and/or overall preference. Frequently, tangible added-value components are quickly copied so companies and brands strive to develop intangible ones that are uniquely ownable and more difficult to replicate.

Addictive Consumption

This is a physiological and/or psychological dependence on specific products or services. Consumers have been known to be addicted to every possible type of product, but addictive consumption more often refers to drugs, alcohol, gambling, and tobacco. It must be noted, however, that the vast majority of consumerism is not addictive but habitual, and based on individual choice.

Adoption

This term represents the decision by a consumer to buy a product or use a service. The consumer weighs available information and makes a considered choice, which implies a level of repeat use that may result in brand or service loyalty.

Advertising

Advertising is the communications that take place between a company and its target audience using any or all of the paid-for mass media. The process usually employs the services of various agencies, such as branding and design consultancies, full-service advertising agencies, market research firms, and

media-buying groups. Advertising is employed to inform target markets of available goods and services; used to remind consumers that existing brands continue to be available; and designed to create awareness and encourage loyalty. Advertising is also used to reassure consumers that their buying choice was the correct one, known as post-purchase rationalization.

The practice of advertising has been classified as informative, persuasive, or manipulative and has led to debate on its effectiveness and efficiency. This debate has created a notable shift from advertising in mass media campaigns to increasingly targeted activities that can more credibly claim results while being less intrusive in consumer's daily lives. The debate has also driven a trend toward integrated marketing, reflecting the broad mix of communication channels currently available.

Advertising Wear Out

This is the point when consumers become indifferent to an advertising message because of overexposure; it's when repeated viewings no longer have any effect. Also called *consumer wear out*, this can often result in a backlash against the offer, which is the complete opposite of the original intent.

Affinity Marketing

This is a form of loyalty development or customer relationship management designed to cement the emotional bond between consumers and brands. It centers on an exchange of information that enables consumers to learn about brands, while companies gain insights into consumers. Unlike loyalty marketing, affinity efforts do not represent an economic exchange, although third parties may benefit, such as consumers rewarding charities based on credit card points. Affinity marketing may also take the form of helplines, membership clubs, newsletters, chat rooms, and so on.

Agency of Record

A designation assigned to the primary communications agency responsible for some or all of a company's or brand's media planning, buying, and creative duties. It denotes an ongoing relationship, and implies legal "agency" responsibilities, that is, the ability of the agency to represent the client to providers and sellers of media services.

AIDA Model

This is a "hierarchy of effect" model that stands for **a**wareness, **i**nterest, **d**esire, and **a**ction, the four successive stages a buyer passes through while making a purchase decision. The model itself refers to a working format for charting consumer attitudes and buying behavior.

Aided Recall/Brand Awareness

A line of questioning used in market research that prompts respondents about specific communications, brands, or services. It is designed to determine any or all associated recall and awareness, and differs from *unaided recall* during which respondents are questioned without any specific prompts. See Brand Awareness and Recall

AIO's (Activities, Interests, and Opinions)

These are variables used in psychographic consumer research to organize individuals into specific segments. The variables used for the segmentation are **a**ctivities, **i**nterests, and **o**pinions, and this research is designed to understand buyer behavior rather than just pure demographics. See Psychographic Segmentation

Notes:

Alignment

Alignment is achieved when employees understand and demonstrate a company's brand and its values through their behavior and actions. It is an increasingly critical aspect of branding as it ensures that the brand experience matches and aligns with the promises made through external communication. Employees are recognized and rewarded based on their adherence to brand objectives so that consistency, a key aspect of branding, is delivered.

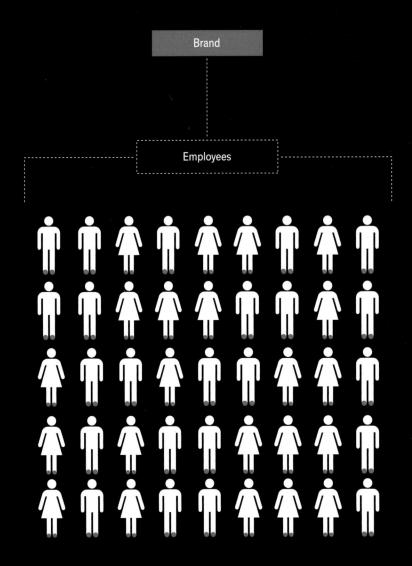

A

Alphanumeric Naming

The practice of assigning letters and numbers to differentiate brand names among versions of products. These products are often related, and the alphanumeric system communicates a hierarchy of value and/or delineates product relationships. For example, models of cars often have alphanumeric names as evidenced by the BMW car naming system.

Ambassadors

These are individuals who represent a brand but are not directly tied to marketing communication functions. Every employee is expected to live the values of the brand, but brand ambassadors go a step further and promote its values throughout the organization even though they may work in finance, operations, logistics, and so on. See Champion

Analytics

In business, analytics is a term used for sophisticated forms of business data analysis. In marketing and branding, a variety of statistical and non-statistical methods are used. The valuation of branding and marketing activities is becoming increasingly topical. Brand valuation, return on brand and marketing investment, and brand scorecards are being introduced as prescriptive tools for improved business performance. These promote better decision-making and add scientific support to areas which have largely been guided by intuition and past experience.

Anchor Store

This is a major retail store that serves as the prime attraction for shoppers in a mall. There are often two anchor stores, placed at either end, intended to encourage large numbers of customers to visit the mall, and to generate traffic for all the stores in the facility. Mall branding can rely on the image of the anchor stores but runs the risk of overreliance if those stores were to leave that location.

Annual Report

This is a yearly record of a publicly held company's financial condition that is presented at its Annual General Meeting for approval by shareholders. It normally includes a profit and loss statement, a description of the company's operations, a balance sheet, and a report from the company's auditor and president. An annual report is designed for investors to understand a company's current status and future plans. This publication often acts as a corporate brochure so the content and design are reflections of the brand.

Architecture

See page 8

Art Director

In the advertising and branding worlds, an art director is responsible for the look and feel of a print ad, brochure, company logo, or interactive campaign, and, in a TV commercial, for its visual style. Traditionally, an art director's counterpart is a copywriter who, obviously, writes the words. Either or both of them may create an original idea for a brand that develops into some form of customer communication.

Notes:

Architecture

Brand architecture is how a company structures and names its brands and how all the brand names relate to each other. Architecture is a critical component for establishing strategic relationships, and there are three types: monolithic, where the corporate name is used on all products and services offered by the company; endorsed, where all sub-brands are linked to the corporate brand by either a verbal or visual endorsement; and freestanding, where the corporate brand operates merely as a holding company, and each product or service is individually branded for its target market. There are multiple variations of these three primary structures. The key requirement is that any architecture be devised with the customer as primary focus, rather than by internal influences such as accounting, people organization, or history.

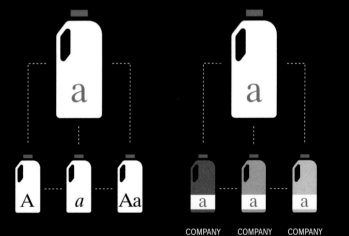

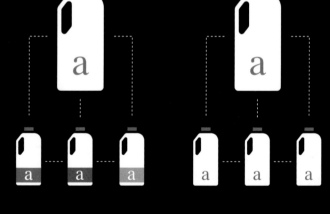

COMPANY I   COMPANY II   COMPANY III

Holding Company
The product/service brands stand alone with limited connection to the corporate brand.

Endorsed
The product/service brands are prominent with an endorsement from the corporate brand.

Maker's Mark
Both corporate and appropriate product/service brands are used with the emphasis on the product brands.

Masterbrand
One brand to identify all products/services and descriptors to unique product competencies.

A

Brand Fact:
80 percent of companies believe they deliver a superior customer experience, but only 8 percent of their customers agree, according to Bain & Company.

Artwork

Digital files of a design or logo that are ready for print or production. Design work will be artworked following design approval. The artwork file ensures the correct size specification, resolution, colors, fonts, and optimum layout before handing over for print or production.

Asset

Something that possesses attributable value and earning potential for its owner. There are three asset types: current, fixed, and intangible.

Associations

The positive and negative feelings, beliefs, or knowledge consumers have about a brand, whether purchased or not. These associations are formed by mass media, word of mouth, trial use, and/or repeat use. Positive ones are leveraged, while negative ones are often difficult to overcome once they have taken root.

Attitude

A lasting, but general, evaluation of an object. Attitudes may cover brands, products, services, organizations, advertisements, innovations, ideas, issues, activities, opinions, and individuals, and they are formed by what consumers hear and what their actual experience is.

Attributes

Attributes are characteristics of a company, product, or service. They can be either positive or negative and can be functional (what a product does) or emotional (how it makes a person feel). Attributes are measurable and can be benchmarked versus important competitors. If attributes are what a brand has, then benefits (what the brand does for a customer) are why certain attributes are important. Much market research is focused on understanding the most important and powerful attributes of a product, service, or brand.

Modern	+	I like to be cool
Inspirational	+	I want the best
All-American	+	I'm buying national
Functional	+	I like being practical
Esthetic	+	I feel like a million dollars

Audience Measurement

This is surveying consumers' media habits, including viewing, reading, listening, and usage. Audience measurement tracks trends and takes place over time or at marked intervals. The resulting insights have historically been based on behavior tracking, but now include monitoring consumer satisfaction. The objective is to determine attitudes and adjust products and services accordingly.

Audit

An audit is a comprehensive, systematic, independent, and periodic examination of an organization's performance. A *brand audit* specifically verifies performance, internal and external communications, customer experience, and so on. The results identify performance gaps, competitor advantages, and market opportunities. An audit is a blend of art and science employing quantifiable and qualitative data based on business and brand strategies.
See Qualitative and Quantitative Research

Awareness

Awareness is the degree of a consumer's knowledge about a specific brand. There are both quantitative and qualitative research techniques used to determine consumers' ability to identify a brand versus competitors in sufficient detail to make a purchase. Brand awareness is a common measure of the effectiveness of marketing communications. Unaided awareness is spontaneous, while aided or prompted awareness is when a brand is recognized among others that are listed or identified.
See Aided Recall and Brand Awareness, and see Qualitative and Quantitative Research

Brand Fact:
On average, prices of private-label goods of all sorts are approximately 27 percent below branded products, based on research from Information Resources Inc.

Regard your good name as the richest jewel you can possibly be possessed of – for credit is like fire; when once you have kindled it you may easily preserve it, but if you once extinguish it, you will find it an arduous task to rekindle it again. The way to gain a good reputation is to endeavor to be what you desire to appear."

Socrates

Notes:

....

....

....

....

....

....

....

....

....

....

....

....

....

....

....

....

....

Balanced Scorecard

A technique originated by authors Kaplan and Norton for measuring business performance. It is based on evaluations of financials, markets/customers, internal processes, and organizational learning and growth. The model is being adopted and adjusted for brand management and measurement. The quadrants are adjusted to make it more specific to the brand or general communications.

Banner Advertisement

This is an announcement that stretches across the entire width of a printed or website page. It is either static or animated and, on web pages, often offers a click-through to access further information.

Barrier to Entry

Any defendable factor a company can use to fend off competitors is called a barrier to entry and they can be legal, natural, sunk investment, tactical, good business practices, or brand. The expression can also refer to the costs for someone new to enter a marketplace.

Barrier to Exit

A company's inability to withdraw from certain markets or actions, or to redeploy associated resources to more valuable activities. It may be difficult to withdraw without retiring a portion or the entire initial investment.

Basic Elements

These are the essential tools that build a visual identity. They consist of a name, logotype, symbol, typeface, color palette, style of imagery/photography, and tone of voice. Each of these elements is combined to create an identity system for a brand.

BCG Matrix

Originated by the Boston Consulting Group, this construct has been widely adopted to explain and guide portfolio management. It was originally developed to chart entire businesses or divisions, but it is now being applied to customer segments, brands, product groupings, geographies, and so on.

Behaviors

The obligatory behaviors that underpin the brand platform and values. These behaviors have meaning at the corporate and individual level and their adoption will ultimately determine the speed (and/or likelihood) of cultural change.

Belief

Belief is a descriptive thought people have about a product, service, innovation, idea, issue, company, or person – whether or not they've had direct interaction with any of them. Belief and attitude can be confused because they're often used interchangeably, but an attitude is evaluative while a belief isn't.

Below-the-line Communications

This is a term used for communications that don't involve the purchase of media. With communications becoming more integrated,

B

this and *above-the-line* communications are becoming less and less accurate descriptors. Below-the-line activities may include publicity, direct marketing, promotions, and media relations.

Benchmarking

Benchmarking is a performance comparison. The most typical form takes place versus competitors or within specific industries. Its origins are in manufacturing, but it has been adopted in other industries, functions, and specific measurements. Benchmarks can be misleading if not taken in their proper context or in concert with additional variables that demonstrate a more complete picture of the situation being examined.

Benefit Segmentation

A method of dividing (segmenting) markets based on what individual groups want from a brand. For example, the market for beer might include a segment for light beers, another for dark beers, another for pale ales, another for imported brands, and so on.

Best Global Brands

This is an annual performance report on the economic value of the world's leading brands produced by Interbrand employing a proprietary methodology. Expressed in dollars and as a percentage of market capitalization, the report ranks the top 100 brands using publicly available data on brands with values greater than US$2 billion and which have significant sales outside the country of origin. Public relations firm, Burston-Marsteller, conducted a study on which rankings global CEO's pay attention to and the Best Global Brands was number three. Interbrand also conducts over ten country-specific brand rankings including France, Taiwan, and Brazil.

Boilerplate

A largely consistent set of written communications that is repurposed multiple times. Boilerplate is often used to produce collaterals or for frequent and similar responses to requests for proposals. Considered a timesaver and consistency tool, boilerplate is also dangerous as it may be overly generic or inaccurate for certain audiences and purposes.

Bottom-up Planning

This is when senior management request plans from more junior departments or managers for inclusion in corporate or marketing planning. The process is meant to inspire less senior levels to achieve performance targets since they are actively involved in the planning process. It is the opposite of top-down planning, where goals and objectives are set by senior management and are handed down through the ranks to be achieved.

Brainstorming

After an issue or opportunity is presented, stakeholders, subject matter experts, and/or completely objective participants are organized to have a "brainstorming session," a free-form discussion designed to achieve consensus about a solution and required next steps. Various methods of facilitation are employed to manage the process and its success often depends on the skill of the facilitator.

Brand Fact:
McDonald's has over 30,000 eateries globally. Starbucks has over 9,000 with a plan to expand to 30,000 based on sales projections and potential geographic locations. The ubiquitous coffee shop opens 3.5 stores per day.

Brand

A brand is a mixture of attributes, tangible and intangible, symbolized in a trademark, which, if managed properly, creates value and influence. "Value" has different interpretations: from a marketing or consumer perspective it is the promise and delivery of an experience; from a business perspective it is the security of future earnings; from a legal perspective it is a separable piece of intellectual property. A brand is intended to ensure relationships that create and secure future earnings by growing customer preference and loyalty. Brands simplify decision-making, represent an assurance of quality, and offer a relevant, different, and credible choice among competing offerings.

Brand Awareness

Brand awareness is commonly used in marketing communications to measure effectiveness. It investigates how many target customers have prior knowledge of a brand as measured by brand recognition and brand recall. Brand recognition (also called *aided recall*) measures the extent to which a brand is remembered when its name is prompted; for example, "Are you familiar with the Sony brand?" Brand recall (also called *unaided recall*) refers to a customer being able to remember a specific brand when given a category of products without mentioning any of the names in the category.

Brand Book

A unique articulation of the brand in both words and visuals which brings the brand and its story to life. Usually directed at internal audiences, brand books are now developed to tell the brand's story for all constituents fulfilling a pledge to be consistent in execution.

Brand Brief

This is the planning document for any brand-building project. It sets out the goals, objectives, competitive landscape, current capabilities and performance, timelines, and budget. It ensures that all stakeholders are aligned to anticipated change and that a sound business case is in place to make any significant changes to the brand.

Brand Commitment

The degree to which a customer is committed to a given brand in that they are likely to repurchase/reuse in the future. The level of commitment indicates the degree to which a brand's customer franchise is protected from competitors.

Brand Culture

The Interbrand practice and overarching process of ensuring that the employees of an organization are the first audience to be exposed to and deeply understand what the brand is meant to achieve. Incredibly, for many years, the internal audience was the last to know about the brand, and that caused performance issues as these were the individuals who were meant to deliver on the promise made through external communications. This specialty within branding goes far deeper than internal communications and launch events. It involves human resource practices encompassing rewards and recognition, compensation, and career path development.

Brand Cycle

The process Interbrand uses to create and manage a client's brand as a valuable asset. It outlines the breadth of services and associated benefits. It commences with an evaluation of an existing brand or the creation of a new one and takes the owner through a robust strategic and creative series of interventions meant to deliver a clear return on brand investment.

Brand Earnings

These are the profits that can fairly be attributed solely to a brand. They result from the revenues the brand generates, and are distributed by dividing the profits between all assets or parties

Notes:

that contribute to generating it. This profit split approach is the most widely used and recognized method for assessing the economic value of a brand and is employed by the majority of accountants and consultants. It is also becoming the standard accounting method for capitalizing goodwill on the balance sheet.

Brand Equity

Brand equity is the sum of a brand's distinguishing qualities, and is sometimes referred to as *reputational capital*. A product or service with a great deal of brand equity enjoys a competitive advantage that sometimes allows for premium pricing.

There are different definitions of the term in different markets. In the UK, brand equity is mainly used to describe market research-based measurement and tracking models that focus on consumer perceptions. In the US, it is used for both research and financially based evaluation models. These models use consumer research to assess the relative performance of brands. They do not provide a brand's financial value, but they do measure consumer behavior and attitudes that have an impact on a brand's economic performance. Some models add behavioral measures such as market share and relative price.

Brand Equity Insights

A quantitative evaluation of the three components that comprise the equity of a brand: knowledge (familiarity, awareness, relevance), distinction (personality of the brand), and commitment (credibility, loyalty, satisfaction). This proprietary research methodology from Interbrand produces an understanding of the market structure and the factors that drive loyalty and commitment within that structure.

Brand Essence

The brand's promise expressed in the simplest, most single-minded term. For example, Volvo = safety; AA = Fourth Emergency Service. The most powerful brand essences are rooted in a fundamental customer need.

Brand Experience

See page 16

Brand (or Product) Extension

This is the use of a well-known brand to launch a new product into a different segment of its overall market. For example, Jello went to market with Jello Instant Pudding as a brand or product extension. The benefit of this strategy is clear through leveraging existing equities, however, if the extension is too far away from the original category it may actually impact the reputation and value of the original brand.

Brand Guidelines

Within companies, everyone involved in building and maintaining a successful brand uses brand guidelines. They are designed to inform and motivate, and are critical in establishing and reinforcing a strong internal brand culture. Guidelines can include vision and values, design and writing requirements, strategy and positioning statements, and even a company directory of how to contact a brand's key managers. The guidelines are part enforcement and part motivation to ensure a consistent execution of the brand. They provide full information and empower staff and third-party suppliers to successfully develop the brand independently.

Brand Licensing

This is a brand owner leasing the use of its brand to another company, most often for a fee or royalty. Though an attractive stream of revenue, it is important for the brand owner to ensure that the equities of the brand are protected so that the licensee does no damage to the brand over the term of the agreement.

Notes:

Brand Experience

The means by which a brand is created in the mind of a stakeholder. Some experiences are controlled, such as retail environments, advertising, products/ services, websites, and so on. Some are uncontrolled, like journalistic comment and word of mouth. Strong brands arise from consistent customer interactions that combine to form a clear, differentiated, holistic experience.

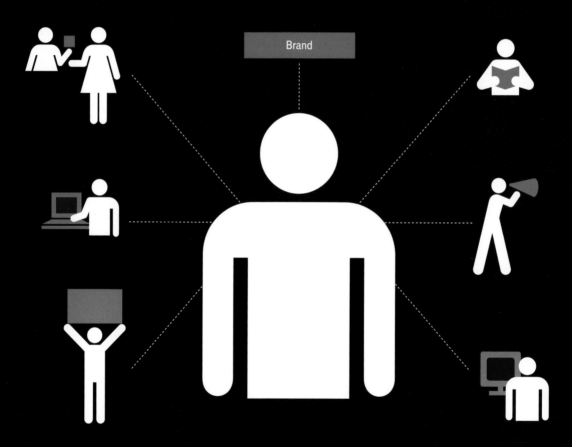

Brand Fact:

The International Chamber of Commerce estimates that the counterfeiting industry comprises 5 to 7 percent of global trade and is worth roughly US$450–500 billion.

Notes:

....
....
....
....
....
....
....
....
....
....
....
....
....
....
....
....
....
....
....
....

Brand Management

The process of managing a company's brands to increase long-term brand equity and financial value. It was originally invented and championed by Procter & Gamble as a competitive system for managing individual brands within a portfolio. Today, however, it is defined more widely and encompasses strategy, design, and deployment of an organization, product, or service. Organizations are increasingly investing in branding for competitive advantage, and this is forcing re-examination of traditional marketing departments, resulting in more responsibility for the chief marketing officer or senior marketing executive. Sophisticated branding organizations employ brand values as guideposts across all functions, ensuring consistent behavior, decision-making, and performance.

Brand Manager

An individual responsible for the performance of a product, service, or brand. The brand manager may also oversee a portfolio of brands, aligning them for maximum effectiveness; ensuring they aren't compromised by tactical errors; and designing crisis management plans. He or she may report to a more senior member of the organization such as a vice president or chief marketing officer.

Brand Platform

An Interbrand construct for positioning that outlines the goals of an organization, product, service, or brand. A brand platform calls for a deep understanding of what differentiates a brand and makes it credible and relevant to defined target audiences. It also requires informed decision-making regarding a brand's ability to stretch beyond its initial category and competition. The platform comprises:

- Brand vision: the brand's guiding insight
- Brand mission: how the brand will act on its insight

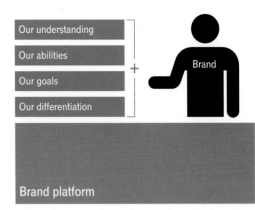

Brand platform

- Brand values: the code by which the brand lives. The brand values act as a benchmark to measure behaviors and performance
- Brand personality: the brand's recognizable and ownable personality traits
- Brand tone of voice: how the brand communicates to its audiences.

Brand Positioning

Positioning is the unique, strategic location of the brand in the competitive landscape. It establishes communications to consumers in a way that sets it apart from the competition, ensuring that consumers can differentiate between it and others. Basically, positioning is the place in the marketplace that a brand's target audience believes it occupies through the offer of tangible and intangible benefits.

Brand Positioning Statement

This serves as a company's internal guide to its marketing communications strategy concerning an individual brand. It sets out the benefits and associations that set the brand apart from its competition in a meaningful way. A brand positioning statement includes the words, pictures, and/or images that create a common understanding, and aligns beliefs and actions.

Brand Protection

Brand protection refers to the legal steps taken to register the uniqueness of a brand and protect it as an asset. Pepsi-Cola has registered its product formulas, packaging shapes

Brand Valuation

Brand valuation assesses the financial value of a brand. Although there is a wide range of methods available, the "economic-use" approach is now the most widely recognized and applied. Economic use assesses the value of a brand by identifying its future earnings and discounting them to a net present value using a discount rate that reflects the risk of those earnings being realized. The economic-use approach was developed by Interbrand in 1988. The methodology integrates structured market and brand assessment with rigorous financial analysis.

These valuations drive management decision-making in many areas; optimized business investment, portfolio management, licensing, tax planning, litigation support, and mergers and acquisitions transaction support.

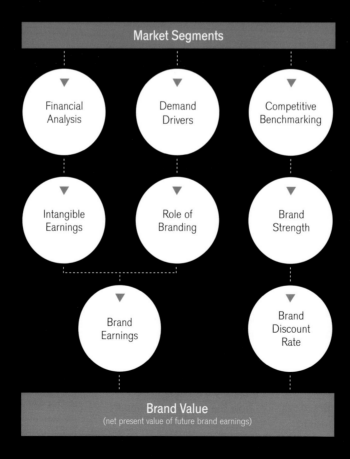

> If this business were split up, I would give you the land and bricks and mortar, and I would take the brands and trademarks, and I would fare better than you."

John Stewart, Former CEO, Quaker

Brand Fact:
Forrester Research found that word-of-mouth, viral, or buzz marketing reaches up to 46 percent of North American consumers.

and designs, website addresses, advertising slogans, and so on, to ensure that it protects all Pepsi's associated distinctiveness.

Brand Strategy

Brand strategy is a "big picture" plan, a clear vision and articulation of how a brand will deliver distinctive and relevant benefits to target customers. An effective brand strategy answers five critical questions:

1. What are the most profitable customer segments to which the brand must appeal?
2. What is the single-minded value proposition that is going to compel these high priority customers to repeatedly choose the brand?
3. Why should these high priority targets believe in the brand?
4. What are the facts that support the value proposition?
5. How do we communicate and implement the branding, marketing, and operational plan so employees and sales channels will adopt it?

There is no prescription or template for developing a brand strategy. Many different models exist, but all should be rooted in the brand's vision and driven by the principles of differentiation and sustainable customer appeal. And they must be based on specific industry and competitive variables.

Brand Strength

A portion of Interbrand's brand valuation methodology, this is a detailed assessment to decide if the brand's forecast earnings will be realized. A discount rate is determined based

on the risk premium for the brand. This results in the net present value of brand earnings.

Brand Tango

Brand Tango is a proprietary approach to consumer branding developed by Interbrand. Its intent is to generate breakthrough ideas by applying best practices from winning brands outside a client's category to inspire fresh thinking. It is accomplished through the repeated and multiple pairing of brands in symbiotic, yet often unexpected, combinations. Brand Tango itself takes its inspiration from the Argentinian tango. The tango is a dance executed with passion and style, where each movement is carefully choreographed and the outcome of each dance is uniquely dependent on the interaction and synergy of the two individuals dancing. This makes it the perfect metaphor for an approach to innovation: inspired combinations of brands for breathtaking results.

Brand Valuation

See page 18

Brand Value

This is the dollar premium resulting from customers' commitment to a brand and their willingness to pay extra for it as compared to a generic offering in the same category. It is the financial worth attributable to the brand, and it

Brand Fact:

Consulting magazine cites the three main reasons why clients select consultants: understanding of specific needs, depth of functional expertise, and depth of industry experience. Price was fourth.

Notes:

....

....

....

....

....

....

....

....

....

....

....

....

....

....

....

....

....

....

demonstrates the value of the brand (or portfolio of brands) as part of a corporation's intangible assets.

Brand Value Calculation

Brand value is the net present value (NPV) of the forecast brand earnings, discounted by the brand discount rate. The NPV calculation comprises both the forecast period and the period beyond, reflecting the ability of brands to continue generating future earnings. This calculation is part of the proprietary Interbrand valuation method and helps determine the effect of marketing strategies, communication budgets, return on brand investment, and other key business and brand decisions.

Brand Value Management

Interbrand's methodologies for creating and managing brand value. This is a comprehensive array of services and tools employed to position a brand now and into the future. The goal is to ensure loyalty from defined target audiences to deliver economic benefits to the brand owner.

Brand Values

The small number of descriptive behaviors that the brand is to exemplify. These are to represent the company, brand, and employees. Examples include passion, inventiveness, respect, honesty, and/or collaboration.

Brandchannel.com

Brandchannel.com was established in February 2001 by Interbrand and is an online magazine committed to providing a global brand perspective. *Brandchannel.com* publishes original articles and papers on a weekly basis, and challenges readers to think about the important issues that affect brands now and that will affect them in the future. To further enhance brand awareness, the magazine offers tools and information, including conferences, courses, and careers worldwide, and links to other valuable industry resources.

Branding

This is the strategic and creative practice of creating brands and managing them as valuable assets. See Brand and Brand Management

Business-to-business Branding

This is brand building and communications involving inter-business buying and selling. The substance of the communications focuses on relationships, account management, and solutions. Sales cycles tend to be longer and more complicated since the size of the transactions tends to be large. An example would be a technology consultant selling a large systems integration program to a global financial services organization.

Business-to-consumer Branding

This is brand building and communications involving consumers. Although this activity has traditionally employed mass-market communications, business-to-consumer brands are now using more targeted communications for effectiveness and efficiency.

Buyer Behavior

This is the action taken by consumers during the purchasing process, which includes consideration, trial, repeat purchase, and loyalty. Understanding the thought processes of prospective and existing customers allows organizations to tailor their offers and communications to facilitate purchase decisions.

Buzz

See page 21

Buzz

This is a term that refers to media and public attention about a product or service. If there's a great deal of buzz, the brand managers are doing something right … but if the silence is deafening, then it's back to the drawing board. *Buzz marketing* is based on this phenomenon, and relies on people passing along product information and recommendations to family and friends. *See* Viral Marketing

"The aim of marketing is to know and understand the customer so well that the product or service fits him and sells itself."

Peter F. Drucker

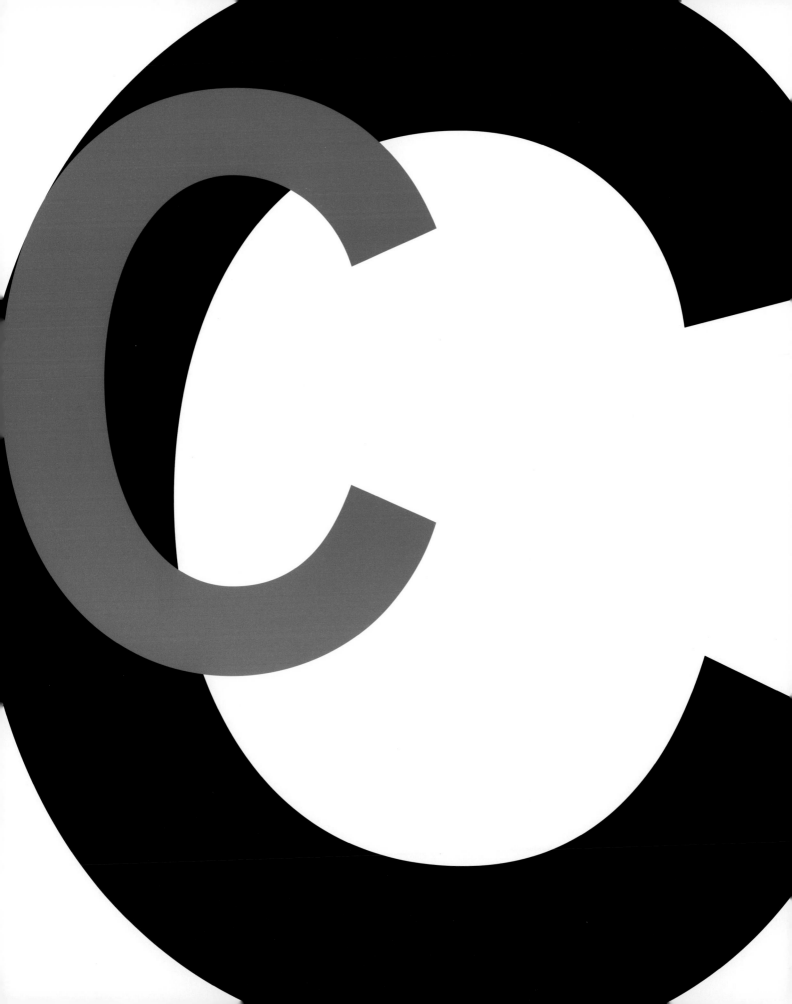

Brand Fact:
The *New York Times* reports that 80 percent of all global brands now deploy a strategy for the "tween" segment.

Cannibalization

What is called cannibalization occurs when a brand extension or line extension takes sales away from existing and established brands owned by the same company. Overlap between brands is not unusual, since consumer segments within a product category tend to have some commonality. But the risk in this overlap is that higher margin brands may be negatively affected by lower margin ones, resulting in overall losses of revenue and brand value.

Category Management

Credited to Procter & Gamble, this system was introduced in the 1980's as an improvement over brand management. In brand management, managers are very entrepreneurial and pay little attention to competition with other brands owned by their company in the same or related categories. On the other hand, category management broadens managers' responsibilities so they are responsible for the category's and the brand's overall financial well-being. They manage cannibalization (see above), optimization, and cross-promotion situations.

Cause Branding

Cause branding relates to a for-profit organization aligning itself with a charitable cause to share mutual benefits. The cause is generally an existing nonprofit organization that shares values, beliefs, and audiences with the for-profit. This is often the most visible act of corporate philanthropy and social responsibility. With the increasing sophistication of consumer response to shallow communications, alignment with a nonprofit organization must be a strategic and long-term commitment on behalf of an organization, service, or product.

Challenger Brand

A challenger brand is a non-market leader that makes a strong effort to take market share away from its competitors, or a brand that already has a strong presence but is trying to take over the leadership position.

Chain of Experience

All individual and potential touch points a customer can experience when interacting with a brand. These involve all five senses and must be managed holistically to ensure that the brand promised is the brand delivered. The chain of experience is frequently modeled to determine benefits prior to investment.

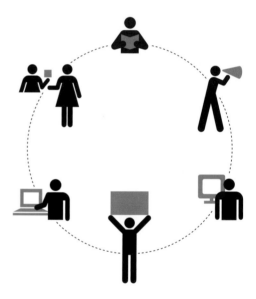

Champion

One step beyond brand ambassadors, brand champions are individuals within a company who spread the brand vision and values and cultivate the brand within their organization. This informal role varies from stimulating awareness, to cases where the champion tries to move a project forward despite the existence of entrenched internal resistance. The more employees a company can turn into brand champions, the better it will be equipped to build and maintain strong brand equity. For example, Harley Davidson, Nike, and Google all have well-deserved reputations as companies with strong brand champions.

See Ambassadors

C

"

A house of brands is like a family, each needs a role and a relationship to others."

Jeffrey Sinclair, Brand Strategist

Notes:

Channel of Communication

The three primary components of any communications program are message, audience, and channel. Channels are communication vehicles and they include websites, brochures, sales forces, television, radio, newspapers, public speaking, publishing, and so on. Choosing the appropriate channels is a significant part of any communications strategy, plan, and execution. Channel choice is meant to determine the most efficient and effective means of reaching target audiences with specific messages.

Chief Marketing Officer (CMO)

A relatively new title in the corporate hierarchy, the CMO generally has responsibility for all external communications and holds primary responsibility for brand management execution. It is widely believed that the chief executive officer should "own" the brand but the CMO ensures strategic, creative, and consistent execution of the brand strategy.

Choice

Choice is the decision made by consumers to select a particular brand from a range of brands with similar features, benefits, and costs. A *choice set* is the final group of brands from which consumers choose, and a *choice model* is an effort that tries to understand how consumers use and combine information about various products or services so they can choose among them.

Clutter

The sheer number of advertisements and messages competing for consumer attention in the same medium or place is referred to as "clutter." In order to rise above the clutter and showcase product and service benefits, more innovative and targeted forms of activities are necessary. The traditional media are often no longer enough to effectively penetrate for awareness and choice.

Co-branding

This is a strategy that leverages together two or more brands to form a more compelling offer than either could alone. In order to be successful, however, the two brands must be complementary and jointly promoted to consumers identified as most likely to benefit from the arrangement.

Cognitive Dissonance

The state of anxiety or unease that follows a decision to purchase and creates a need for reassurance that the decision was correct is called "cognitive dissonance."

Collateral

This is marketing and sales promotional print material. Collaterals are often synonymous with brochures that communicate relevant information to target audiences in order to increase awareness, promote purchases, and/or provide post-purchase validation.

Color

Color is an emotional and subjective component of every company's design and communications. Without even being aware of it, consumers make purchase decisions every day based on their attitude toward color. People tend to identify with certain colors and marketers use color to identify a brand, set a mood, communicate specific associations, and differentiate one brand from another.

Brand Fact:
Frank Perdue's chicken slogan, "it takes a strong man to make a tender chicken" was translated into Spanish as "it takes an aroused man to make a chicken affectionate."

Commodity

In economic terms, commodities mean all goods and services. In branding, however, a commodity is a product or service that tends to compete solely on its functional attributes. Brands create tangible and intangible associations which allow for significant differentiation from alternatives and, therefore, greater security, revenue, and profit.

Communication

Communication is transmitting and exchanging information by writing, speaking, electronic means, and the like. It is also the process of establishing a commonly understood meaning of facts, thoughts, and opinions between senders and receivers.

Communications Audit

A review of the portfolio of internal and external communications in terms of their look and feel, tone of voice, and consistency of message, visual or otherwise. This provides an insight into the current strengths and weaknesses in communications and where the opportunities lie for future communications.

Community

A brand community is everyone inside and outside a company who is somehow involved with building a brand, from internal departments, suppliers, and the media, to customers, prospects, and advertising and public relations agencies.

Competitive Advantage

This is the above-average performance of a company, product, or service that results in additional profits. These additional profits are typically reinvested to maintain continuous advantage over competitors.

Competitive Landscape

Almost every brand exists in a competitive environment that is constantly being modified by time and changing consumer preferences. Effective brand management requires brand owners to examine their brands regularly, and to understand that future threats may not come from brands on the radar screen now, but those that will become challengers in the future.

Competitor

Competitors are brands that are vying with each other for success in the same market – brands that are considered viable alternatives by consumers because they can provide satisfaction almost equally well. *Competition-oriented pricing* is when a company decides on a price based more on what a powerful competitor charges than on consumer demand or production costs.

Competitor Analysis

This analysis is usually focused on a company's closest competitors. The goal here is to understand the resources, practices, and results that set a competitor apart. These can then be emulated, countered, or marginalized, based on strategic actions.

Concept Development and Testing

When potential buyers are shown the description of a new product and asked for their reactions, and then, at a later date, shown a prototype of the product and asked for additional feedback. See Prototype

Conditioning

Various marketing and advertising actions taken by a company to develop and foster a favorable impression of its brand in its markets. Consistent communications are required in order to introduce and educate the consumer concerning the brand and its associated benefits.

C

Every company has its own language, its own version of its history (its myths), and its own heroes and villains (its legends), both historical and contemporary."

Michael Hammer

Consideration Set

This is the array of available brands in a category from which consumers can choose. Consumers form it in a rational and deliberate manner, focusing on the functional aspects of the brands. Once established, the consideration set remains largely stable and follows its own version of the law of diminishing returns where choice is impaired when more brands are added.

Consistency

Consistency has two meanings in branding: first it refers to the implementation of a brand's visual identity and tone of voice across all customer touch points. BMW is perhaps the best example of a brand whose visual identity and tone of voice is implemented consistently around the world – from the correct placement of its logo, to the correct design format of its dealerships. Second, consistency is a qualitative and quantitative measure of a brand's ability to repeatedly deliver the experience it promises to its customers. For example, Coke's product is consistent both over time and internationally, and Apple computers have consistently delivered a user-friendly experience targeted at the creative market.

Conspicuous Consumption

The overt display of a consumer's ability to afford luxury brands is called "conspicuous consumption." The term was developed by American economist Thorstein Veblen and now relates to brands symbolizing a consumer's status in society. Brands as status symbols have recently been extended beyond luxury brands to include icons embraced by brand loyalists, such as Starbucks and Adidas.

Consumer

A consumer is the ultimate user of goods, ideas, or services who acquires for direct use and ownership, rather than for resale or other reasons. The term also refers to the final decision-maker and, in this sense of the word, doesn't differentiate whether a person is a current or potential buyer.

Consumer Choice Model

This is a construct that tries to understand how consumers use and combine information about various products or services so they can choose among them. It identifies a hierarchy of decision-making encompassing benefits, image, price, ease-of-use, and so on.

Consumer-perceived Risks

Word-of-mouth information about a product, service, or brand. They tend to relate to performance issues and can affect a consumer's perception of risk prior to deciding whether or not to buy.

Consumer/Product Relationship

This is understanding how a particular brand relates to an individual consumer's goals and values. Understanding this relationship is basic to developing effective market strategies. Loyalty is the ultimate goal of branding and by understanding this relationship, brand owners can more accurately match brand to buyer.

Notes:

A great brand is a story that's never completely told."

Scott Bedbury

Consumer Products

These are tangible goods produced for final consumers, not for businesses. Typically, consumer products are heavily branded, widely advertised, and distributed through recognized retail channels. Well-branded consumer products condense the decision process for consumers by simplifying choice. However, competition in long-established markets is intense, demanding constant brand revitalization.

Consumer Profile

This is all the distinguishing demographic, lifestyle, and personality characteristics of consumers in a particular market segment. Brand values can be mapped to these distinguishing characteristics for more accurate communications to promote adoption and sustained use leading to loyalty.

Consumer Purchasing Process

This is the entire process a consumer goes through before making the decision to purchase a specific brand. It comprises:

- Awareness (understanding there is such a brand)
- Interest (learning more about its value)
- Desire (comprehending the need for it)
- Action (making the purchase decision)
- Post-purchase evaluation.

Marketers will use different tactics to move consumers from step to step. Specific measures of success must be developed against each step to gain clear understanding of effective and efficient branding and marketing practices.

Notes:

....

....

....

....

....

....

....

....

....

....

....

....

....

....

....

....

....

Conversional Marketing

This is an activity designed to get consumers to change their minds, ideas, or attitudes about a product. This is usually accomplished by offering it at a lower price, or by increased or specially designed advertising and promotion. The term also means converting qualified prospects into active clients.

Cooperative Advertising

This is an agreement between a manufacturer and a retailer to reimburse the retailer in full or in part for placing manufacturer-produced ads and commercials locally, with the understanding that their name will be included in the copy. Co-op advertising can also refer to a joint effort between two or more businesses to pool advertising money for more buying power. In this case, the ads would feature both company names and benefits. From a branding perspective, the quality and image of the two players must be commensurate and offer mutual benefit in communications.

Copy

In a branding context, copy refers to the spoken words in a commerical, or the written words in advertisements, magazines, newspapers, or any marketing communications vehicle. Copy must be compelling, impactful and fast to grasp given the proliferation of communication and messaging in business. Specific to branding, copy must adopt a distinct tone of voice that helps to draw immediate and clear associations with the brand.

Copyright

A legal device designed to protect work/ product from being used without authorization is called a "copyright." It is recognized by its symbol © and guarantees the creator's legal rights. In theory, it automatically ensures creator/owner control, but it demands that the work be in a tangible form; that is, ideas cannot be copyrighted.

C

Brand Fact:
Scandinavian vacuum manufacturer Electrolux used the following in an American campaign: "Nothing sucks like an Electrolux."

Notes:

....
....
....
....
....
....
....
....
....
....
....
....
....
....
....
....
....
....

Copy Testing

An effort to evaluate consumers' reactions to the effectiveness of communication messages. It can happen while a campaign is being developed (pre-testing), during a campaign, or after it has been launched (post-testing).

Core Competencies

Core competencies are what a company does best, a particular set of skills that contributes most to its ability to succeed and enables it to deliver benefits to consumers and achieve competitive advantage. These are generally intangible attributes that are difficult to copy, thus forming a great part of the brand's overall uniqueness.

Corporate Identity

This is a corporation's brand and it is communicated through the combination of the organization's name and its use of visuals (logo/color/artwork). Furthermore, corporate identity includes all an organization's supporting communications elements such as tone, manner, graphic structure, and music.

Council

A permanent working group within a company that guides and manages the building of a brand, evaluates its success or failure, and takes steps to reinforce the former and correct the latter. It should be representative of all internal stakeholders rather than solely representing marketing and/or customer service. The council is most effective when empowered to make change and when it reports to the CMO or equivalent.

Counterfeiting

Occurs when an organization or individual produces an inferior and cheaper product that looks like a branded product and is packaged and presented in a manner to deceive the purchaser. This damages the true brand and

continues to be a significant issue globally. In China, counterfeits of luxury brands like Louis Vuitton proliferate.

Country of Origin

This is the country from which a well-known and supported brand originates. Long-term theory has assumed that a brand is partially evaluated or chosen based on where it's from – fine leather goods from Italy, for example, or timepieces from Switzerland. Current theory, however, is overturning the importance of country of origin as consumers assign more weight to the quality, convenience, and cost of the brand.

Creative Strategy

This is an outline of the brand message companies want to convey to target audiences. It is the set of guiding principles art directors and copywriters follow when creating advertising or marketing communications campaigns. Sometimes, creative strategies are called *brand platforms.*

Credibility

Credibility means that customers believe a brand will deliver what it promises. It is chiefly earned through consistency over a period of time, but it can also be achieved, in the shorter term, by the persuasiveness of communications. Credibility is arguably the most important criterion a brand can have. Any erosion of credibility impacts reputation and equity and will impact the financial performance of a brand.

Crisis Management

A well-rehearsed contingency plan used by companies to respond to unexpected negative events. Its intent is to reduce and control the harmful impact of whatever situation occurs by using every communication vehicle at its disposal. A strong brand can contribute to crisis control by drawing on all the equity accumulated over time to help weather the crisis.

Cult Brands

These are brands that enjoy customer loyalty that has moved beyond simple allegiance and into cult-like devotion. Those who drive their Harley-Davidsons to Starbucks daily may qualify. These devotees tend to live the brand and it forms an integral aspect of their life. These are also known as *tribal brands.*

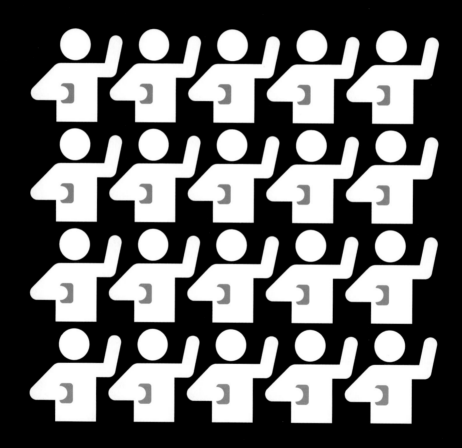

C

"

'I am irresistable,' I say, as I put on my designer fragrance. 'I am a merchant banker,' I say, as I climb out of my BMW. 'I am a juvenile lout,' I say, as I pour an extra strong lager. 'I am handsome,' I say, as I put on my Levi's jeans."

John Kay

Notes:

Critical Behavior Drivers

These are the most important aspects of consumers' buying habits and behavior, and are used by market research companies to predict future trends. These drivers can be mapped to the brand's attributes signaling a clear link between consumer wants and needs and the brand's benefits and associations.

Cross-selling

Cross-selling is encouraging existing customers for one product or service to buy additional products or services from the same company (as opposed to buying more of the same). Not only is cross-selling designed to generate revenue, it is also intended to broaden a customer's reliance on a company and, therefore, decrease the likelihood of their buying from a competitor. This is more effectively achieved if the original product or service has a clear and powerful brand.

Cult Brands

See page 30

Culture

A company's culture is the sum total of the beliefs, history, practices, policies, and activities that define its unique personality. A company's brand is part of its culture and a brand actually has a culture of its own, represented by the people who work for it, their operating style and behavior.

Customer

Often used interchangeably with "consumer," a customer is one who actually purchases a brand, product, or service.

Customer Acquisition

This is the process of using a variety of marketing techniques to gain customers who were previously unaware of a company's products or services. Simply stated, the goal of a customer acquisition program is to transform potentional customers into actual buyers. Convincing a customer to buy is the goal of marketing – convincing a customer to continue to buy is the goal of branding.

Customer Characteristics

Customer characteristics refer to distinct demographic, behavioral, and psychographic features, traits, or facts. They include age, sex, earning power, occupation (demographics); propensity to purchase and repeat purchase (behavioral); and expressed self-image, attitudes about life, and so on (psychographics). Groups of customers who share the same or similar characteristics become a defined customer segment, which can then be effectively targeted with products and promotions relevant to their needs. See Psychographic Segmentation

Customer Defection

Customer defection measures how long a certain customer or group of customers can be expected to remain loyal to a product or service, and the length of time they can realistically be expected to generate income. It is a consideration in calculating lifetime value. See Lifetime Customer Value

Customer Relationship Management (CRM)

This term refers to a technology system and/or a formal program for managing relationships between organizations and customers. The

"We're not concerned about having consistency of brand so much as about consistency of purpose that flows throughout the whole organization. It doesn't actually matter what we write on the napkins or say through advertising, all that matters is that when you go into a Pret shop you get that set of experiences that describes Pret."

Andrew Rolfe, Pret A Manger

Notes:

....

....

....

....

....

....

....

....

....

....

....

....

....

....

....

....

....

....

desired result is extensive knowledge about key customer segments, and customized plans to sell to and service them. CRM is designed to focus on the most profitable customers and facilitate cross- and up-selling. Effective brand managers cull the data from these systems for actionable intelligence that helps guide their brand strategies.

Customer Retention

This term refers to the percentage of customers who continue doing business with a company. It also refers to maintaining an existing customer base by establishing good relations with everyone who buys the company's product.

Customer Return on Investment

This is the value a company receives from investing in the acquisition and retention of customers. A critical component of brand analytics, this calculation helps to determine return on brand and marketing investments.

Customer Satisfaction/ Dissatisfaction

Satisfaction means that the needs, desires, and expectations of customers have been met or surpassed, while dissatisfaction means the opposite. Satisfaction, however, does not necessarily equate with loyalty, since an organization or brand can have one-time satisfied customers.

Customer Service

Customer service is the communication, delivery, and after-sales care of the buying public. In the best organizations, it is the centerpiece of their efforts. It is largely delivered through customer-facing employees but also, increasingly, through customer-friendly technology (such as the telephone or internet). Unfortunately, in many organizations, customer service is a department that only handles complaints or answers questions, so it is usually relevant to only a small number of customers.

Customization

Customization is tailoring products or services to the special and unique needs of individual customer segments. This is a business strategy for engendering loyalty by more accurately delivering relevant products and services.

Brand Fact:
According to Interbrand, the three main tasks for a brand owner are:

1. Embody the brand itself in all words and actions
2. Know the underlying sources of brand value and manage them like any tangible asset
3. Constantly keep the brand relevant and differentiated.

"Marketing is too important to be left to the marketing department."

David Packard

"The more modern nations detest each other
the more meekly they follow each other;
for all competition is in its nature only a
furious plagiarism."

Charles Dickens

Notes:

....
....
....
....
....
....
....
....
....
....
....
....
....
....
....
....
....

Database Marketing

This is a form of direct marketing that uses
technology and customer (or potential
customer) databases to generate personalized
communications meant to promote a product or
service. Database marketing emphasizes statistical techniques to develop customer behavior
models, which are then used to target ideal
customers. This form of marketing requires a
significant commitment to maintaining the
accuracy of data.

De-differentiation

De-differentiation is a relatively new phenomenon that describes the breakdown of
traditional barriers between once-distinct
industries. De-differentiation, or *convergence*,
is when multiple industries form alliances or
whole new businesses with the objective of
better serving customers.

Demographics

This is a term referring to statistics relating to
a population and generally covering sex, age,
marital status, birthrate, mortality rate, income,
education, and occupation. Demographics are
still commonly used to identify potential
customers, but are often augmented by
more specific methods that help understand
buyer behavior.

Design

See page 37

Design Elements

The individual components comprising the
overall visual expression of the brand. These
can include images, type, color, shape, texture,
and so on. These elements work in cooperation
with each other to communicate an overall
brand personality and image.

Design Principles

The set of objectives and parameters that guide
consistency in brand development. These
ensure that equities are retained while allowing
some creative license to extend the brand's
visual vocabulary.

Design to Cost

In the development of new products, this is an
approach that considers cost as its own design
consideration, rather than as the outcome of a
completed design. Here, costs would be based
on projections about what consumers can
afford and the nature of the competitive landscape. It helps build a business case prior to
significant investment.

Differentiated Marketing

This is a market strategy that aims to take the
same brand to several market segments at the
same time but varying the marketing mix for
each segment. It takes into account that each
segment is unique so that the message and
channel will require adaptation based on preferences and norms.

Differentiation

This is the process of identifying, branding,
and communicating the actual and emotional
benefits that make a product or service unique
versus competing, but seemingly similar,
choices. Differentiation is at the heart of
branding to simplify choice by providing
tangible and intangible benefits to guide
the decision-making process.

Design

As a verb, design refers to the process of creating and executing a plan for a new product, service, or idea. As a noun, it refers to two things: to the final result of the plan (in the form of a model, sketches, blueprints, or other descriptions), or to the finished, produced product itself. Design in all forms is a powerful method and component of brand building – it can differentiate, more effectively communicate, and position a brand in its competitive environment.

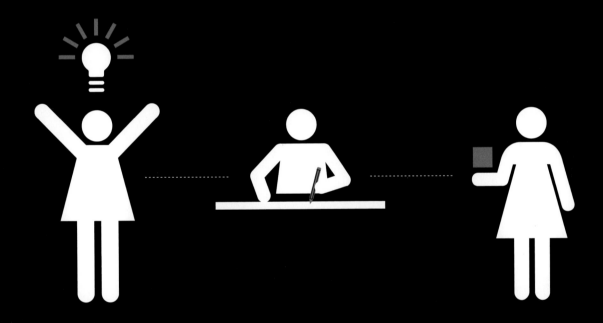

"Anyone can look for fashion in a boutique or history in a museum. The creative person looks for history in a hardware store and fashion in an airport."

Robert Wieder

D

Differentiator

A differentiator is the aspect of a company, product, or service that separates it from the competition. It could be a performance difference (facts and figures, for example), or an emotional one (the imagery and associations of the company or offering). It was once thought that only one differentiator was required to ensure competitive advantage, but current thinking expresses differentiation as a bundle of multiple differentiators that, when presented in combination, provide true advantage.

Digital Brand Management

This is a response to the complexity and speed required to manage truly global brands. In the past decade, there has been a proliferation of digital brand management tools meant to control consistency and distribution of brand assets. These take the form of intranets, application service providers, and fully outsourced systems. Initially, this was simply the automation of traditionally printed brand guidelines, but the tools have grown to encompass image libraries, packaging templates, advertising templates, and so on. These systems work best in widely distributed organizations where many people communicate the brand strategy to audiences. It allows the brand to be controlled, yet also allows it to evolve as it touches the market. A leading provider of these products and services is BrandWizard.

Direct Marketing

This is a form of marketing that sends messages directly to consumers, using "addressable" media like mail. Direct marketing, therefore, differs from regular advertising in that its messages aren't placed in third-party media (like radio, TV, or billboards by the roadside). Direct marketing is attractive to many marketers because, in many cases, its effectiveness can be measured directly. In contrast, measurement of other media must often be indirect, since there is no direct consumer response. While many marketers like this form of marketing, it is sometimes criticized for generating unwanted solicitations, which are sometimes referred to as "junk mail" and "spam." Direct marketing uses various channels — coupons, catalogs, mail, consumer and business magazines, newspapers, telephone, and radio to convey an offer that is intended to elicit an almost immediate response. Direct marketing is comprised of a definite offer, all the necessary information upon which to base a purchase decision, and a response mechanism that consumers can use with limited effort or expense.

Discontinuous New Product

A term often used to describe a new innovation — a product that departs significantly from previous products in the same area. These new products are often found in technology, where entirely new markets are created rather than just extending existing ones.

Diversion

A genuine product is sold to a buyer in one market/channel and then resold by the same buyer into another market/channel, without the consent or authority of the brand owner, in order to take advantage of a price arbitrage situation. This definition also applies to *parallel trade*, *gray market* or *gray market activities*.

Domain Name/Address

The part of an URL (commonly pronounced "earl") that specifies the source of a website or email. The domain name in http://www.interbrand.com/services.asp is www.interbrand.com. Company names are best to trade under, but product or generic names such as brand-effectiveness.com can also redirect casual browsers to the main URL.

See URL or Uniform Resource Locator

Notes:

Brand Fact:
In the 2005 Best Global Brands ranking, the top 10 brands were worth a combined US$390 billion.

> Companies that enjoy enduring success have core values and a core purpose that remain fixed while their business strategies and practices endlessly adapt to their changing world."

James Collins

80:20 Rule

This is an oft-quoted rule of thumb stating that 80 percent of sales (or 80 percent of profits) come from 20 percent of the customers.

End-of-aisle (or End-cap) Display

This refers to coveted positions for package goods marketers in retail stores. As the name suggests, these are displays placed at the ends of aisles where they are prominent and very visible. End-of-aisle displays generally provide dramatic increases in spontaneous purchase or take-away.

Endorsed Brand

A brand that carries the endorsement of a source brand (the parent company), for example Chips Ahoy! Here, Chips Ahoy! promises a specific taste profile and experience, while Nabisco (the source brand) offers an endorsement of overall quality, heritage, and food expertise. The source brand is leveraged to communicate value or expertise that strengthens the promise of the endorsed brand.

Essence

Essence is a collection of intangible attributes and benefits, the core characteristics that define and differentiate a brand. The easiest way to understand essence is to imagine that the brand is a person you are trying to describe — what defines that person, and what separates her or him from everyone else.

Every Day Low Pricing (EDLP)

This is a retail strategy meant to create consistent customer traffic based on low prices. EDLP grew in importance as Wal-Mart's ability to negotiate low prices from suppliers became one of their main core business strategies. Short-run pricing strategies such as seasonal or special event sales often confuse and irritate consumers, while EDLP provides clarity and consistency in the shopping experience.

Notes:

Brand Fact:
There are over 886,000 members of the company-sponsored Harley-Davidson Owners Group. They organize rides, training courses, social and charity events.

An exercise of modeling projected customer interactions that sum their overall experience when dealing with a brand. It details all possible touch points, frequencies, and situations to ensure that the brand will not disappoint. This is a sophisticated process that manages risk and reward while identifying new areas the brand to outperform competitive offers.

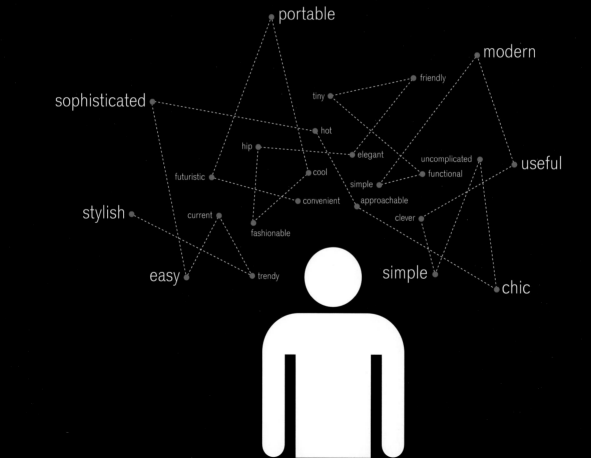

E

"Show me a great company and I'll show you one that has radically changed itself and is looking forward to the opportunity of doing so again."

Lawrence Bossidy

Exclusion Zone

The area around an element such as a logo that must remain clear. It is documented in the design guidelines with associated rationale. Also referred to as clear space, free space, control area, and keep-free zone.

Expectation

Expectation is the idea that even before trying a brand, consumers have already formed an opinion about it. These expectations are the minimum threshold the brand must exceed. If it doesn't, customers will be disappointed and apt to be vocal to other prospective customers, negatively influencing their purchase decision.

Experience

This is when consumers have been exposed to various brand attributes. A successful brand experience happens with exposure to a brand's most positive aspects, and this can happen in a store, through advertising and websites, or through word of mouth. The critical aspect is to have the experience match or exceed the customer's expectations based on promises made in communications.

Experiential Mapping

See page 44

Experiential Marketing

An approach that tries to evoke a strong emotional response in potential buyers about a product or service. Typical examples might be tourism commercials that show beautiful beaches and dramatic sunsets, or diamond communications that suggest romance and eternal love.

Extension

This is the act of using an existing (and successful) brand name to help launch a new product or service into a new area or category. Since the original brand has strong, positive associations and high levels of awareness, the decision to use it involves risk, because if the new venture fails, it may tarnish the original brand.

Notes:

"Word of mouth is the best medium of all."

Bill Bernbach

"Creative thinking may simply mean the realization that there is no particular virtue in doing things the way they have always been done."

Rudolph Flesch

Flanker Brand

This is a product introduced by a company into a market in which it is already established. The intent of a flanker brand is to increase overall market share in a particular category and aggressively crowd out the competition.

Focus Group

This is a group of people assembled to discuss an issue, idea, or product. Focus groups are a staple of market research, and their success usually depends on the quality and experience of the facilitator.

Four P's (Product, Price, Promotion, Place)

This is a widely taught concept meant to explain the vital components of marketing. However, it is now known as oversimplified shorthand, because the Four P's have been extended to include additional P's, among them pre- and post-customer service. See Seven P's

Franchise

A franchise is a legal contractual relationship between a supplier and one or more independent retailers. The franchisee gains an established brand name and operating assistance, while the franchiser gains income as well as some control over how the business is run.

Freestanding Brands

These are brands that companies use when they want to maximize the impact of a portfolio of brands by leveraging the strength of each one with little or no connection to a source brand or other (often competing) brands from the same company. As examples, Pantene and Pert Plus are freestanding brands from Procter & Gamble that are in the same shampoo category.

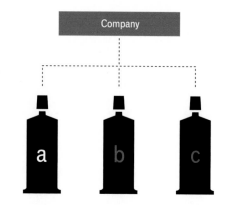

Notes:

Brand Fact:
Multi-channel customers spend 20 to 30 percent more money, on average, than single-channel ones do, according to McKinsey & Company.

Brand Fact:

12 percent of companies spend 75 percent or more of their budgets on customer retention, according to Tivoli Partners and Interactive Marketing & Research.

Brand Fact:
Spencer Stuart provided a study that shows average CMO tenure is under 24 months.

Notes:

....
....
....
....
....
....
....
....
....
....
....
....
....
....
....
....
....

Gap

Every company develops business strategies for its brands, and every consumer experiences these brands individually. A brand gap is the distance, or difference, between the business strategy and the consumer experience. Obviously, companies want that gap to be as small as possible.

Generic Brands

These are unbranded products offered by retailers, usually at a lower cost than similar branded products. Initially, generics were given minimal packaging, advertising, and promotion support but they are now seeing more support and offering greater competition. Consumers have been educated that the quality of generics rivals that of their branded cousins, and larger numbers of customers are purchasing generics, regardless of the lack of premium associations.

Generic Name

This is a brand name that has become associated with a product category rather than with a particular brand. Kleenex for tissue has been widely noted as the most obvious example of generic naming.

Generic Strategy

Michael Porter, from Harvard Business School, developed the theory that there are three basic strategies for any organization – cost leadership, differentiation, and focus. Porter initially argued that an organization must focus on one of these to achieve an advantage. More recently, however, both anecdotal and empirical evidence demonstrates that it is a combination of the three that helps organizations succeed.

Global Branding

See page 53

Goodwill

An intangible asset comprising brand value and other assets, such as customer service and employee morale, that are anticipated to represent higher earning power. The drawback is that goodwill does not have a generally recognized liquidation value and accounting principles require that it be written off over a specific time period.

Gradient

The progression of a specific color into the next complementary color.

Graphic Design

Graphic design is the process of arranging words and images to communicate a message or clarify understanding, and it can appear in almost every communications medium, from newspapers, magazines, and digital, to movies, animation, and packaging. Successful graphic design takes into account target audiences and the message hierarchy meant to be conveyed. Creativity and differentation are sought to stand out amongst competing communications and firmly gain awareness in the market. Graphic design is an invaluable aspect of branding.

Grid Systems

This refers to the design and structure of information that should be followed. Also referred to as page layouts, style templates, image grids, and templates.

Global Branding

A global brand is one that is available in many nations and, though it may differ from country to country, the local versions have common values and a similar graphic identity. These are branding initiatives that are consistent, yet are tailored to local languages, customs, business practices, and buying behaviors.

"Well-managed brands live on – only bad brand managers die."

George Bull

Your brand is created out of customer contact and the experience your customers have of you."

Stelios Haji-Ioannou, Chairman, EasyGroup

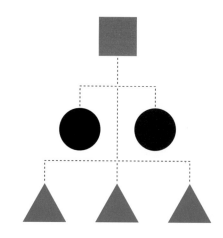

Harmonization

Ensuring that all products in a particular brand range have a consistent name, visual identity, and, ideally, positioning across a number of geographic or product/service markets.

Harvesting

Harvesting is when sales of a brand begin to decline and companies slowly reduce their marketing investment, either to nothing, or to a bare minimum. These companies depend on the brand's loyal customers to sustain it while they free up cash to pursue other opportunities. Brand harvesting usually precedes a brand's total elimination.

Hero Pieces

A selection of communication pieces that show how best to use the visual identity that can be referred to as best practice examples. These are profiled in the brand guidelines and are often never static as the brand and its visual and verbal components evolve to maintain and enhance relevance and differentation.

Hierarchy

Simply stated, hierarchy is the order of things — what comes first, next, and after that. This term can be applied to brand architecture (that is, corporate name, division, and operating unit); to organizational structure (who reports to whom); or, most interestingly, to needs (that is, it's more important to customers that we quickly resolve their issues rather than that we achieve 100 percent compliance).

Homepage

A homepage is the first page or screen you see on a website. It is the site's entry point and is intended to greet visitors, supply information about the site or its owner, and provide a "table of contents" that leads visitors to linked supporting pages. It is another opportunity for the brand to communicate its distinct benefits graphically, in copy, and interactively.

Notes:

....
....
....
....
....
....
....
....
....
....
....
....
....
....
....
....
....

Brand Fact:
66 percent of executives say true ROI analytics are marketing's greatest need, according to Booz Allen Hamilton.

"Brand equity is the sum of all the hearts and minds of every single person that comes into contact with your company."

Christopher Betzter

Brand Fact:
79 percent of brand professionals surveyed on Brandchannel believe the "Made in China" label hurts Chinese brands. The top three association notes were: cheap, poor value, and poor quality.

Notes:

Icon

An icon is the symbol of a brand that is deeply entrenched in the minds of consumers. Tony the Tiger, the Harley-Davidson crest, and the Nike "swoosh" are all brand icons that are indelibly etched into the conscious and subconscious minds of consumers. Icons are tremendous assets with incredible value, however, they require regular updating to infuse them with new and relevant meaning.

Identification Decisions

These are choices a company makes about the branding identity it wants to give to a product. Typically, the choice is from among four alternatives – single brand names (Cheerios), product-line brand names (Quisinart cookware), corporate brand names (Scope mouthwash) and corporate family name (Knorr soup).

Identity

The outward expression of a brand. This includes everything from its name and visual appearance to the way it sounds, feels, smells, and tastes. The brand's identity is its fundamental means of consumer recognition and symbolizes its points of difference. It represents a unique set of associations which affect how a brand appears in consumers' minds. Identity, however, is a strategic goal (while image is a consumer's actual perception of a brand). The goal, obviously, is for identity and image to be the same.

IDMetrics

A proprietary quantitative and qualitative Interbrand research methodology that seeks to assess the existing and potential visual identities of brands in terms of appropriateness, credibility, and strong positive and negative associations, as well as fit-to-concept. Points of relevance and disconnect are identified with the brand audiences, as well as the fit and stretch of each identity with the brand strategy.

Image

Image is the overall impression and unique set of associations a company or brand communicates to the public. It is achieved through advertising, websites, brochures, annual reports, logos, symbols, and so on, and although it's not always factual, it is very powerful. The term gained popularity when research began to make it clear that image influences consumer purchases.

Image Library

Stock shots are photographs, illustrations, and video and film footage available for use by anyone for a set fee or, if they are in the public domain, for free. An image library is either a company in this business for profit, or non-profit organizations (like a library, for example) that offer stock shots as a public service.

Impact Model

See page 61

Impression

The technical definition of impression is the total number of exposures to an advertisement in a specified period of time. This is a measurement used to determine if a desired target audience is absorbing and reacting to a specific ad.

Impact Model
A proprietary Interbrand construct that links brand strategy with creativity and implementation. The model sequentially answers four fundamental questions – who, what, why, and how? Who are the high priority targets that will drive profit and growth? What is the single-minded aspirational brand promise? Why should the target believe the promise – now and in the future? How do we internally and externally bring the value proposition? The model has recently been expanded to include a fifth question – how much? The last question quantifies the results of the entire effort so involves a return on brand investment component.

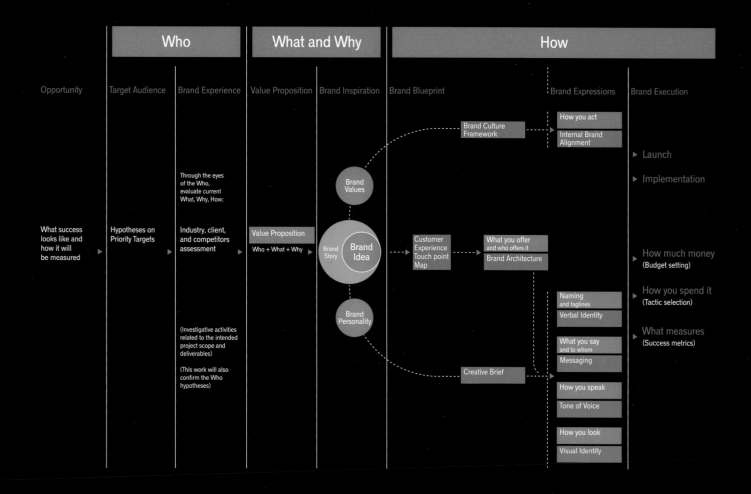

Brand Fact:

IDC CMO Advisory researched the
Top 5 Marketing Measurement
Mandates from the CEO:

- Consistent metrics for ROI of
  marketing
- Measurement of brand awareness
  and reputation
- Consistent lead-generation metrics
- Improved tracking and
  measurement of marketing
  spending
- Programs that lead to increased
  revenue.

Impulse Buy

This is a spontaneous purchase made without
prior deliberation or investigation into the
benefits of the product or service. It is often
associated with goods made available at
checkout counters.

Inform–Engage–Align

See page 63

Innovation

Any new approach to designing, producing, or
marketing can be called an innovation. Innovations usually provide the innovator with an
advantage over the competition because they
can supply new products based on established
demand, or open up new markets. Inherently,
innovations are highly differentiated, allowing
them to be successfully branded.

Innovation-based Culture

In a marketing sense, innovation means intro-
ducing new products, ideas, or services into the
marketplace; new products that are different, or
that consumers perceive to be different. These
new products can either be the next step in an
existing product's evolution, or a new product
entirely. Innovation is an essential component of
a company's long-term growth, and an
innovation-based culture is one in which
everyone understands this to be true and works
toward it as a goal. Communication innovation
is critical to branding to ensure the ongoing
relevance of the brand to desired audiences.

Intangible Assets

Intangible assets like goodwill, trademarks,
patents, management expertise, brands, copy-
rights, formulas, and so on, have no physical
substance, nevertheless, they are perceived as
crucial in creating value. Increasingly the
majority of business value is derived from

intangibles, and brands are one of the most
important of them because of their far-reaching
economic impact. Brands have a powerful influence on customers, employees, and investors,
and in a world of abundant choices, such influence is crucial for commercial success and
creation of shareholder value.

Until recently, intangible assets weren't recognized on the balance sheet, as most of them
were generated internally and therefore lacked
a perceived objective market valuation. The rise
in the value recognition of intangibles came
with the continuous increase in value gap
between companies' book values and their
stock-market valuations, as well as sharp
increases in acquisition premia in the late
1980's. This led to the recognition of the value
of intangible assets in business combinations.
Today, most accounting standards require the
recognition of acquired intangible assets on the
balance sheet.

Integrated Brand Communication

This is ensuring the efficiency and effectiveness
of a brand and marketing mix to convey a
specific message to a desired audience. It is
both a process and a plan that considers the
needs of the target audience, the key messages
to be imparted, and the most appropriate
channels to communicate them. The channels
can include sales, promotion, public relations,
advertising, and so on.

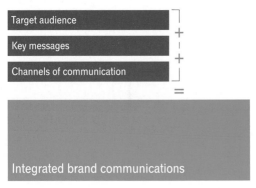

Target audience
Key messages
Channels of communication

Integrated brand communications

Inform–Engage–Align

An approach employed by Interbrand to achieve internal brand alignment. It consists of three primary phases:

- Inform – where employees receive communication regarding the brand that gives them a first-level understanding
- Engage – where understanding gives way to action and demonstration so employees believe in the brand
- Align – where the brand values and objectives are entrenched in business process and human resource practices to encourage the employees to live the brand.

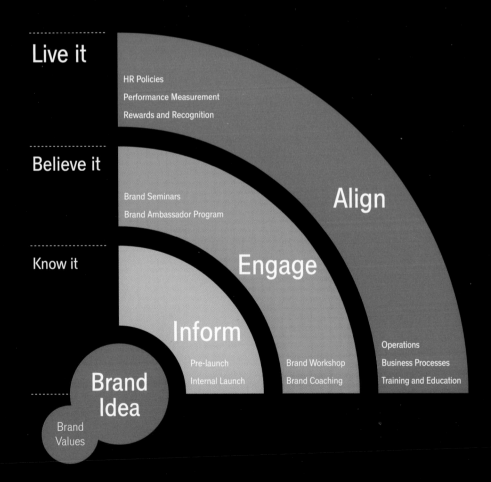

Good customers are an asset which, when well managed and served, will return a handsome lifetime income stream for the company."

Philip Kotler

Notes:

....

....

....

....

....

....

....

....

....

....

....

....

....

....

....

....

....

Integrated Marketing Communications

This is managing all marketing communications (advertising, sales promotion, public relations, and direct marketing) as one cohesive whole rather than as a series of individual activities. This integration assures the clarity, consistency, and maximum impact of a brand's message.

Intellectual Assets

These are non-physical business assets that can include expertise, knowledge, patents, research and development programs, and knowledge-management systems.

Intellectual Property

Intangible assets such as a patent, trademark, or copyright whose value results from knowledge, discovery, invention, or creativity. Intellectual property can cover new products like software, books, reality game show formats, television rights to sporting events, or even a manufacturing process.

Interactive Marketing

This is a method that combines traditional marketing principles with internet techniques so that customers can interact with whoever sends them a marketing or selling message. The interaction can be asking a question, filling out a form, or making a purchase. If a company doesn't have this specific kind of marketing capability itself, it can work with a consultancy that has expertise in web design and development, internet advertising and marketing, and e-business consulting.

Interviewing

Interviewing is asking questions to obtain ideas, information, or opinions, and an *interview study* is a common marketing research technique designed to gather data. The people asked to participate typically complete a written questionnaire, answer questions over the phone, or are interviewed face-to-face.

Investor Relations

This is both an activity and a department in most medium-to-large public companies. It provides existing and potential shareholders with accurate information about the company and its financial performance. This helps investors make informed buy or sell decisions. Over the past few years, investor relations departments have embraced the power of branding to appeal to the investment communities and more accurately represent the value of their companies and brands.

Brand Fact:
Omnicom Group is the largest marketing organization in the world, according to *Advertising Age*, with revenue of US$10.4 billion in 2005.

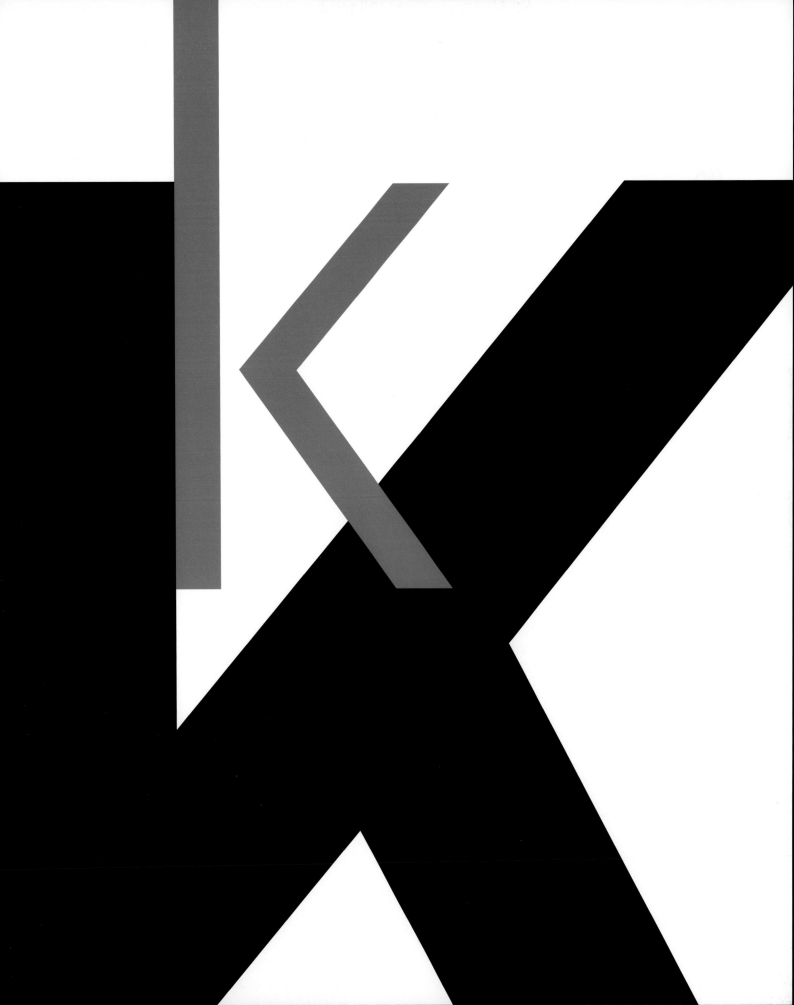

Brand Fact:
There are over 25,000 products
in the average supermarket.

Notes:
....
....
....
....
....
....
....
....
....
....
....
....
....
....
....
....
....
....

Jargon

Jargon is using complicated terms instead of their simple common-use equivalents, and marketers are as guilty of using jargon as anyone. Typically, people using jargon are either trying too hard to sound knowledgeable, or trying to increase their own perceived competence by confusing others.

Jumble Display

A mixture of products or brands from different companies placed on a single display, such as a clearance table. It is this practice at retail that has driven many brands to provide their own in-store displays and product training to remove the risk of the brand being presented inappropriately.

Key Buying Influences

Many factors influence a consumer's decision whether to buy a product or not. There are external factors like the group a consumer feels part of, a specific current situation, and the culture as a whole; internal factors like attitude, lifestyle, personality, and perception; and marketing factors, including the product itself, its price, promotion, and distribution. In addition, many of these facts are interconnected and work together to affect the ultimate buying decision.

Key Performance Measures

These are a focused set of metrics that drive specific management functions. In branding, these metrics may include volume and value of market share, awareness, return on specific branding investment, and so on. Ideally, the key performance measures form a balanced set and are both objective and subjective, and qualitative and quantitative. Also, unless they influence management decisions, they are of little use to the business and the brand.

Knowledge Management

This is the process of capturing, organizing, analyzing, interpreting, and disseminating information and knowledge possessed by individuals in an organization to the organization as a whole. New technologies have aided this process enormously through use of intranets, databases, and communication tools that automate the entire process. Knowledge management systems are entirely dependent upon the quality, timeliness, and frequency of contributions made by individuals. Once, knowledge was power – now knowledge shared is even more powerful.

"The purpose of pricing is not to recover cost but to capture the value of the product in the mind of the customer."

Daniel Nimer

Brand Fact:
The Newspaper Association of America says the average American is exposed to between 1,500 and 3,000 brand messages every day.

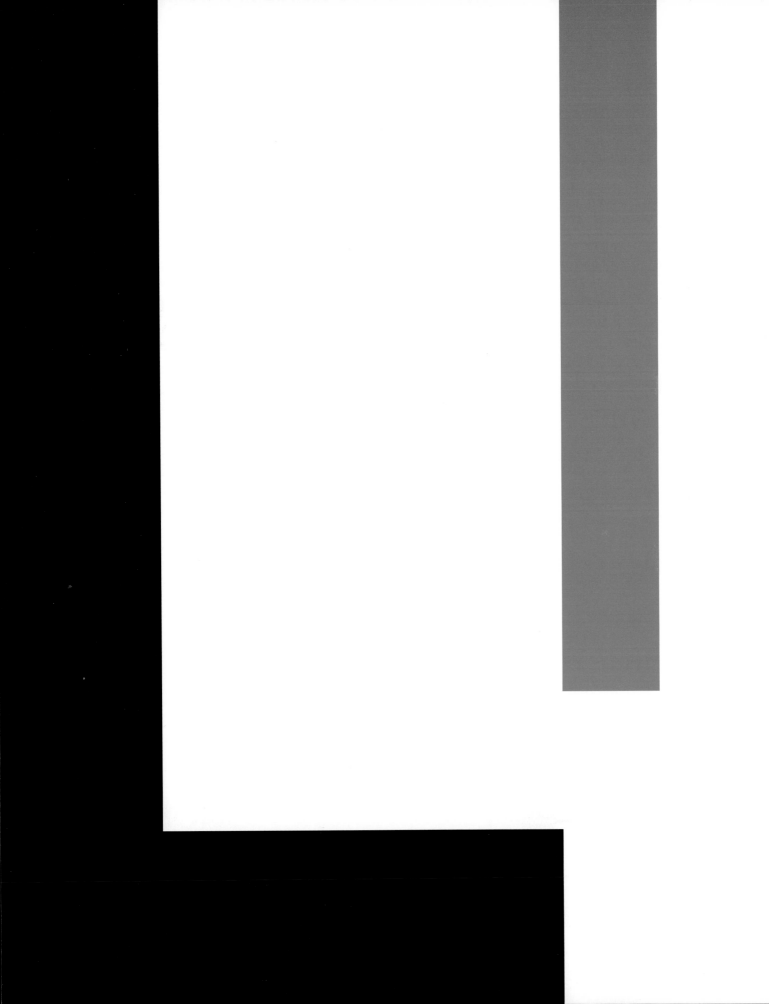

Brand Fact:
Women buy or influence the purchase of 80 percent of today's consumer goods, according to Hitbox.com.

Notes:

Label Graphics

These are the designs and illustrations on any packaging that carry information about the product. For example, its name, use, features, benefits, and so on.

Launch

The time when a company starts to promote a new product or service using advertising, publicity, internal branding, or initial product sales. Launches can be significantly visible, with large budgets and a single starting date, or they can be "soft" and take place over a longer period of time (usually two weeks to one month). Even though soft launches may have smaller budgets and make less "noise," they can still be quite effective. See Rollout

Letterhead

This is a sheet of official company stationery with a printed heading at the top that usually contains the company's name, address, telephone and fax numbers, and often includes a logo and other details.

Leveraging

This is when a company uses the power of one of its successful brands to support one of its new products entering a different, but related, market. Consumers have strong opinions about a brand's quality, consistency, and value, which they often transfer to a "leveraged" brand. For example, consumers who are loyal to a certain computer might be willing to try that same brand's new printer.

Lexicon

In a general sense, a lexicon is an inventory of words — a dictionary, for example. It's the same with this glossary, except this lexicon is specifically an inventory of branding, naming, marketing, e-commerce, design, and communication words.

License

A license is a document or agreement giving permission to do something on, or with, someone else's property. Between two businesses, it is a contract in which one company is given a fee to provide technology, knowledge, or a product to another.

Lifestyle Brand

This is a brand targeted at an audience based on how they live, and it identifies itself with their interests and activities, wants and needs, likes and dislikes, attitudes, consumption, and usage patterns. The attributes of a lifestyle brand are tailored to specific audiences in order to achieve early adoption and sustained use.

Lifetime Customer Value

See page 73

Lifetime Customer Value

This is an equation and approach that calculates a customer's value over that customer's buying lifetime. The goal is to identify the most profitable customers and organize them into specific segments. Then, incentives can be offered to ensure loyalty. It is a calculation about the value of customers to a brand or company over their entire life cycle. This removes the emphasis on individual transactions, and allows companies to focus on very narrow target markets. To calculate lifetime value, the following have to be taken into consideration: how much it costs to acquire the customers; how much it costs to retain them; their average lifetime; and the average value they will provide during that period.

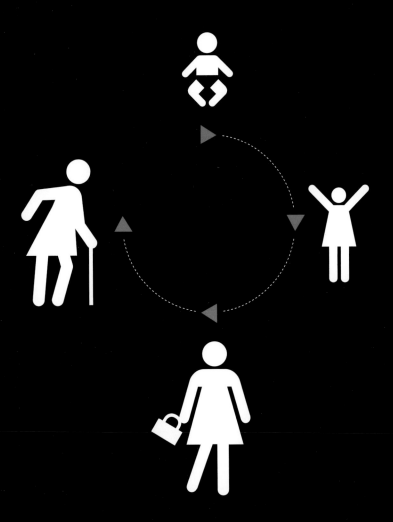

"Quality is remembered long after the price is forgotten."

Gucci family slogan

L

Line Extension

This is the use of an established and successful brand to introduce additional products into its existing category (for example regular Crest toothpaste extending into whitening toothpaste). Line extensions generally offer new features, flavors, colors, packaging sizes, or ingredients. The expected gains are incremental because existing customers will be given more choice and new customers may be attracted.

See Brand Extension

Lock Up

A lock up defines the relationship between two design elements and how the elements should appear together. It recognizes exclusion zones, size and positioning relationships, and rules of independent use. The positioning of a corporate logo with its tagline is an example.

Logo

A logo is the graphic element used to identify a company, service, or product. It is a distinctive mark, sign, symbol, or graphic (usually of the company or brand name) that is in continual use and typically trademarked to protect it from other companies. Logos are immediately recognizable and act as "brand ambassadors" because they become unmistakably identified with a particular organization or brand.

Logotype

Logotype is a company or brand name set in a distinctive typeface or using special lettering arranged in a particular way. In addition, the color and shape of the font should be distinctly different from others in the same market.

Loyalty

Loyalty is the allegiance earned by a brand when it delivers such distinctive and meaningful benefits that customers choose to come back over and over again. It is also the result of satisfied customers recommending a brand to others. Loyalty is successfully making the transition from "a brand I use," to "my brand."

Loyalty Programs

These are specific initiatives that offer an accumulating benefit to consumers who support the brand. They can take the form of point programs, discounts, special offers, select access, or even free goods and services. Frequent flyer and shopping programs are prime examples. (Loyalty programs differ from affinity programs where there is no direct economic value.)

Luxury Brands

Luxury brands are objects or services that are desirable but not essential. They are indulgences rather than necessities and are often expensive or hard to get. Luxury brands often deliver superior quality or better performance and consumers are willing to pay a premium price for them. The challenge of accessing due to either price or supply often results in imitations of the luxury brand.

Notes:

Brand Fact:
Owners of digital video recorders fast-forward through 92 percent of commercials, according to Yankelovich Marketing and Forrester Research.

"It is an immutable law in business that words are words, explanations are explanations, promises are promises – but only performance is reality."

Harold Geneen

Mall Intercept

This is when market researchers in a shopping center stop a sample of passersby and ask if they're willing to answer a few questions. Those who agree then participate in one-on-one interviews to largely determine how they purchase and what drives their loyalty.

Mantra

A mantra is an internally developed short phrase (usually three to five words) that captures the spirit of a brand's positioning. It is usually composed of three terms. For example for Disney, *brand function* is first and this is the nature of the product – entertainment. *Descriptive modifier* is second and clarifies the function – family. Finally, *emotional modifier* describes how the brand provides the benefit, in this case, as fun. So a Disney mantra could be entertainment, family, and fun.

Mark

This is the portion of a brand that consists of a symbol, design, or distinctive lettering or coloring.

Market

The word "market" has various meanings: it is the theoretical and actual place where goods are bought and sold; it can refer to the extent of the demand for a product or service, as in "There is a big market for antique cars"; and it can also refer to the business of buying or selling a specific commodity as in "the soybean market."

Market Attractiveness

This is the measure of profit potential in a given market or industry, taking into account such factors as size, growth rate, and nature of the competition already there.

Market Broadening

Market broadening is a strategy in which a company evaluates the wants and needs of consumers who already buy its product or service in order to decide what else to sell them. For example, a company that sells cell phones might also decide to offer PDA's.

Market Coverage Strategies

There are five different strategies companies typically use to select and target markets:

1. Single market concentration (which focuses on an individual part of the market)
2. Product specialization (which produces a single product for all markets)
3. Market specialization (which produces all products for a single market)
4. Selective specialization (which produces products for multiple market niches)
5. Full coverage (which produces a product for every customer).

Market Crystallization

This is an exercise that identifies parts of a market not yet fully established in order to investigate similar needs people in that market may have for something that doesn't yet exist – and to meet those needs. The result can be to create something entirely new or to expand an existing product or service whose benefits have not been fully developed.

Market Defense

See page 79

Notes:

Market Defense

What a company does to repel the advances of an existing or potential competitor is called "market defense," and there are various available strategies:

1. Building barriers to market entry
2. Increasing entry costs
3. Reducing the market's attractiveness by lowering prices.

If none of these strategies is successful, then market defense gets refocused on minimizing damage.

Build barriers to market entry   Increase entry costs   Reduce market's attractiveness

"About two years ago I realized I was no longer a person but a brand."

Martha Stewart

Notes:

....

....

....

....

....

....

....

....

....

....

....

....

....

....

....

....

....

Market Demand

Market demand is the total volume of a product or service bought by a specific group of customers in a specified market during a specific time period.

Market Diversification

This is a growth strategy in which companies add new products and new markets simultaneously, but products and markets that aren't currently related to their existing activities.

Market Extension Strategy

This is employing a marketing strategy designed for one country and using it to extend into another country, and then another. A *brand extension strategy*, on the other hand, uses the values of a popular brand to expand into new markets or market segments.

Market Followers

These are companies that don't have the resources, commitment, market share, or research and development expertise to challenge market leaders for a more competitive position. Interestingly, these companies can, at times, take advantage of opportunities created by the leaders without having to make a significant marketing investment of their own.

Market Fragmentation

This is when new segments with their own wants, needs, and desires arise out of previously homogenous markets. When this happens, brand loyalty erodes and mass marketing becomes far less useful.

Market Leader

The company or brand that is dominant in its industry and holds the greatest market share. It tends to be on the cutting edge of new technologies or new production processes and has the most flexibility in crafting strategies. Its very visible position, however, makes it the main target of competitiors and, sometimes, government regulatory agencies.

Market Position

Market position is the relative strength of one brand (or company) versus other brands or companies in a specific market. It can be understood as sales versus the competition, or sales as a percentage of the market's total. With knowledge of a brand's position, companies are able to devise strategies to improve it. The descriptive terms often applied to market position are *leader*, *challenger*, or *follower*.

Market Potential

This is an estimate of the size of a market, or the total possible sales of a product or service over a specified period of time. It can also be defined as the market share a particular company can reasonably expect to achieve.

Market Research

This is the systematic approach to collecting, analyzing, and interpreting the information required to make sound marketing decisions. It is designed to determine the potential salability of a product or service by determining what people want and need. The information can be gathered from secondary sources that are already published and publicly available, or from primary sources such as the customers themselves.

M

Market Segmentation

This is grouping a wide assortment of customers in a market into smaller groups based on similar wants, needs, and buying habits. In this way, a car manufacturer, for example, can group younger car buyers with discretionary income into a segment, and then target that segment with sports car advertising and promotion.

Market Share

Market share is the total number of units of a specific product sold (or the dollar value) expressed as a percentage of the total number of units sold by all competitors in a given market. (*Market size*, by the way, is the total dollar amount of possible sales by everyone in that market.)

Marketing

Marketing is the process that brings ideas, goods, or services to the marketplace through planning, pricing, coordinating, promoting, and distribution. Marketing is the process of identifying and reaching specific segments of a population in order to sell them something, and it is also the creation of demand using advertising, publicity, promotion, and pricing. Marketing is an organizational function designed to deliver value to customers and to manage customer relationships in ways that benefit the organization and its stakeholders.

In our society, where nearly all production is intended for a market, marketing activities are just as important as the manufacture of the good or service. It is estimated that approximately 50 percent of the retail price paid by consumers is made up of marketing costs.

Marketing Audit

A periodic and systematic review, analysis, and evaluation of a marketing group's structure, objectives, strategies, organization, goals, action plans, and results.

Marketing Control System

This is the system that checks to see if marketing plans are producing expected results. It measures productivity and profit by types of products, customers, or territories, and measures other key marketing variables such as customer satisfaction. If a product isn't performing as planned, corrective action is taken until it does.

Marketing Cost Analysis

A tool used in marketing planning that examines the costs associated with developing, producing, selling, promoting, and distributing a product or service to certain market segments. It also determines the product's profitability. Additionally, it is an allocation of costs analysis that determines which specific costs are associated with which specific marketing activities.

Notes:

Brand Fact:
In 2003, 43 of the 111 songs in the Billboard Top 20 had lyrics with brand references, according to Datamonitor.

Notes:

....
....
....
....
....
....
....
....
....
....
....
....
....
....
....
....
....
....
....

Marketing Intermediaries

Sometimes called *middlemen*, marketing intermediaries are people and companies who assist the flow of products from the people who make them, to the people who use them. Marketing intermediaries, among others, are financial institutions, agents, wholesalers, distribution companies, and retailers.

Marketing Metrics

Marketing metrics are measurements that help companies evaluate their overall marketing performance, such as market share, advertising and promotion costs, and response rates obtained by advertising and direct marketing.

Marketing Mix

This is a selection of products combined with decisions about price, place, and promotion that a single company uses to pursue desired levels of sales in target markets. This product selection provides options from which customers can choose, and the advantage to the company is that more customers are likely to choose one of their options instead of buying elsewhere.

Marketing Myopia

This term refers to a company's failure to define its goals broadly enough. It is a lack of vision that can result in an overemphasis on a product's specific features and benefits, and an underemphasis on the wants and needs of consumers.

Marketing Planning

This is a systematic process of assessing marketing opportunities and resources and formulating marketing objectives. It is the process that leads to a marketing plan, which is a detailed description (with schedule) of the objectives and actual methods a company intends to use to achieve its marketing goals.

Mass Marketing

This is a process of using the mass media to market widely a product or service to a large target audience. It is based on seeing a market as one homogeneous whole and, therefore, selling the same product, at the same price, via the same advertising and promotion vehicles to everyone. It is designed to sell a large quantity of product to a large number of people.

Masterbrand

This is the principal brand name a company uses for products and services across a business. The masterbrand is usually combined with individual names to make sub-brands. For example, General Electric goes to market with GE Capital, GE Aviation, and GE Financial Services, and companies like BMW and Mercedes Benz go to market in the same way, except they use letters and numbers to differentiate between their various models.

Brand Fact:
In a study conducted by the Keller Fay Group, it was discovered that the average American mentions specific brands 56 times a week in conversation.

Notes:

Measurement

Measurement is determining the extent, size, amount, or degree of something, especially in comparison with a known standard of some kind. In business, the accepted wisdom is: "Don't do it if you can't measure it, and don't measure it unless it either saves or makes you money." All measurements should help businesses make choices and help them to optimize the choices they've made. Marketing will not achieve equal stature with the other business disciplines until it adopts an equally rigorous approach to measuring impact.

Media

Media are all the tools of mass communication, from print (newspapers and magazines) to electronic (radio and television) to computer (websites and so on). *Medium* is the singular form of the word.

Media Buying

Media buying is a service offered by certain advertising agencies that involves negotiating with the various media to purchase time or space to run a client's ads. A *media buy* is the advertising a company pays for.

Media Kit

This is a package of promotional materials distributed by a media outlet in order to sell advertising. A typical kit includes audience demographics, costs, success stories, and related materials – all the information a prospective advertiser needs to make an informed decision.

Media Planning

In media planning, companies analyze their strategic goals and formulate actionable day-to-day tasks to maximize the investments they intend to make in promotion and advertising. The result of this process is called a "media plan."

Merchandising

See page 84

Merger

This is combining two or more corporations into a single entity. Typically one of the corporations survives the other(s) and absorbs all the assets and liabilities. Mergers usually occur in a friendly environment where executives from the respective companies co-operate with each other to ensure a successful outcome. Other times, the merger is "hostile," and a company simply buys the majority of outstanding shares of another company's stock in the open market.

Message–Channel–Market (MCM)

An Interbrand construct that simplifies the intent of branding and marketing communications. In its clearest form commercial communication identifies a desired market for its offer. Then specific messages are tailored to that market to entice members to purchase. Finally, the most efficient and effective channels for those communications to reach and influence the market are selected and employed. The notion of MCM is to simplify and clarify practices that are frequently made more complex than they have to be.

Messaging

Messaging is a concise statement of issues and benefits associated with a product or service. It's the theme that's consistently conveyed through a company's mix of communication channels in order to best reach its target audiences.

Merchandising

Merchandising is a term that has many, generally aligned, meanings. It is the purchase, distribution, and resale of goods at the retail level; it is presenting a product to the right market at the right time using advertising and promotion; it is the attractive and visible presentation of goods within stores; it is also a marketing practice in which the brand or image from one product or service is used to sell another (like NASCAR clothing).

Whenever we have compromised on our principles, we and our customers have been the losers."

Marcus Sieff

Notes:

....

....

....

....

....

....

....

....

....

....

....

....

....

....

....

....

....

....

....

....

Messaging Matrix

A proprietary Interbrand construct which identifies the key audiences for a brand that can act as influencers of larger segments. Those influencers are prioritized based on the brand's objectives and mapped against specific communications that support the overall brand position, yet, appeal to the relevant wants and needs of the audience. A brand cannot be everything to everyone but it must have something for everyone – the messaging matrix is a communications tool that helps articulate that distinction.

Messaging Options

Options for messaging can include testimonials, humor, comparisons, slice-of-life, humanistic appeals, and so on, and are selected to best reflect the values and benefits of a brand. These options are taken into consideration along with the channels that will reach target audiences most efficiently. With an increasing emphasis on integrated marketing communications, messaging options must work across several platforms at the same time in order to achieve maximum effectiveness.

Metrics

In a general sense, metrics are measurements designed to track product development and allow a firm to measure the impact of process improvements. What is measured can include time to market; duration of different process stages; and product development outcomes (such as percentage of total sales due to new products).

Mission Statement

This is an expression of a company's history, managerial preferences, environmental concerns, available resources, and distinctive competencies. It answers the question "What business are we in?" with responses that have broad focus and customer orientation. A mission statement guides a company's decision-making and strategic planning.

Monolithic Brand

See Masterbrand

Multi-brand Strategy

The strategy of a single company going to market with several competing brands instead of one. Companies do this to create internal competition in order to promote efficiencies; to differentiate brands; to sell to different market segments; or to get maximum results out of established brand names. For example, Cadbury sells various chocolate products under different names, and Lever Brothers sells various laundry detergents.

Multi-segment Strategy

This is a strategy that targets a number of distinct segments in the same market and then develops a separate and distinct marketing mix for each.

M

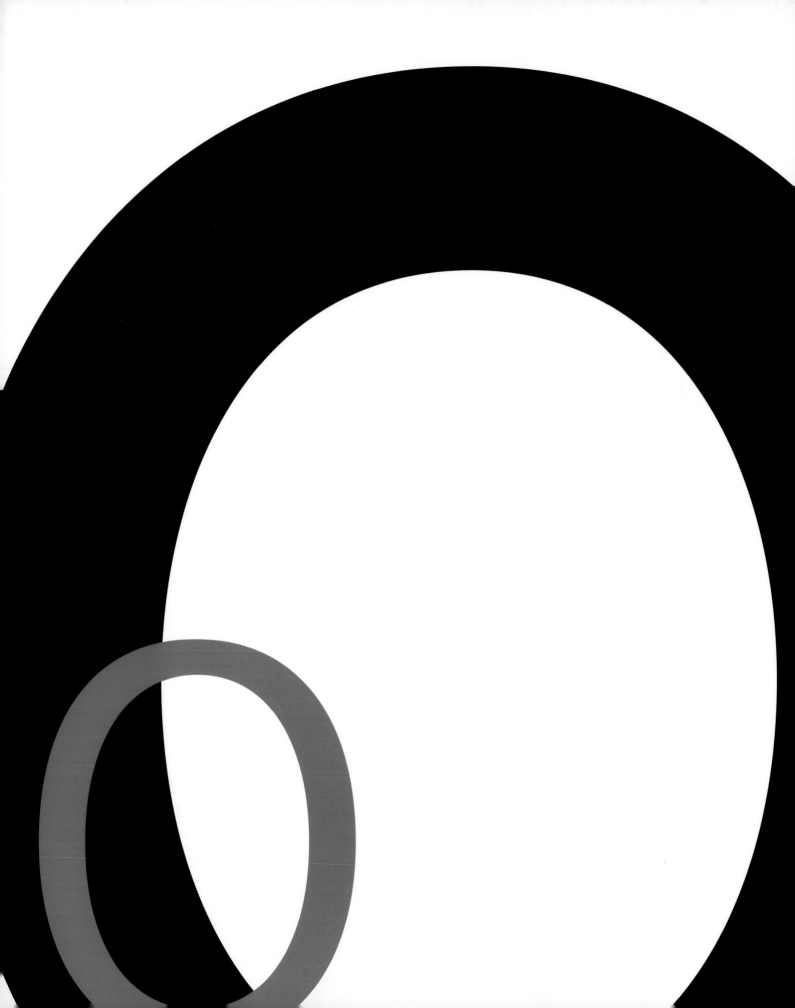

"A well-informed employee is the best salesperson a company can have."

E. J. Thomas

Notes:

....
....
....
....
....
....
....
....
....
....
....
....
....
....
....
....
....
....
....
....

Name

This is the part of a brand that consists of words, letters, or numbers. When the word "trademark" is used, it most often means brand name.

Names

Brand names can be categorized into several name types that relate to the goods or services offered:

- *Descriptive names* use common language that isn't considered trademark protectable to describe the brand's goods and services. They offer the advantage of being transparent in their communication, but they don't often convey much differentiation or emotion. In addition, due to their literal nature, they are difficult to stretch beyond their original use. Examples include Computer Associates, PlayStation, and British Airways.
- *Suggestive names* do not simply describe the benefits of the goods and services associated with them, they also suggest their attributes. They are afforded more trademark protection than descriptive names and often provide more category differentiation and emotion. They can also stretch beyond their original designation. Examples include Oracle, Power-Book, and Crest.
- *Abstract names* – have little or no clear relationship to the goods and services they're associated with, but they can be very distinctive within a category. Once secured, they are offered the highest level of trademark protection and they can also help extend a brand to encompass new products and services. Examples include Orange, Xerox and Blackberry.

- *Coined names* are word combinations that didn't previously exist. They are most often created by combining word roots (often Latin) to create new verbal expressions. For example, the name Prozac is a coined name created by combining the roots of "Professional" and "Exact." Coined names, once secured, make the strongest trademarks.
- *Composite names* are existing words that are combined to create new brand names. JetBlue is an example of a composite name.
- *Real word names* are created by using words that currently exist, but have no obvious link to the product or service they're associated with. Real word names can make strong trademarks. Apple Computer is an example of a real word name.

Naming

See page 89

New Product Development

This is the overall process a product goes through before introduction, and it involves seven phases: idea generation, screening ideas, concept testing, business analysis, developing the product, test marketing, and commercialization. New product development almost always refers to activities within an organization, as opposed to new products acquired from another company.

News Releases

News releases, or press releases, are written or recorded communications directed at the media announcing something purported to have news value. Their intent is to encourage journalists to develop articles on whatever the subject is, and they are commonly used in public relations as a means of attracting favorable attention to the PR firm's client and/or products.

Naming

This is the practice of developing brand names for corporations, products, and services. Most often, the objective of naming is to develop ownable trademarks and trade names that express a brand's promise and provide an easy way for consumers to identify and interact with it. Brand names are valuable economic assets and should be carefully created and protected by their owners.

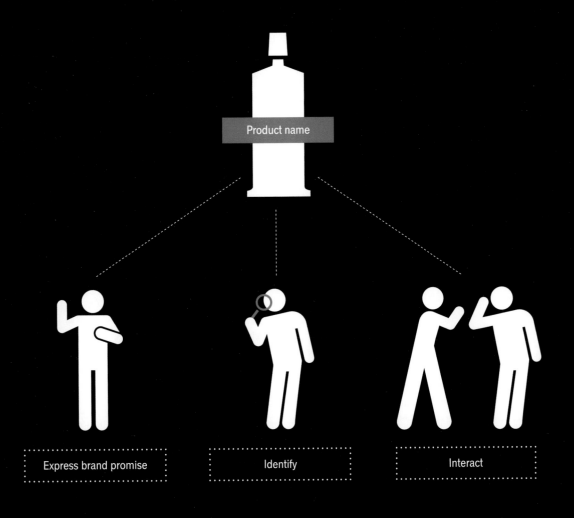

Notes:

Niche Brand

Niche brands are those targeted at individual market segments where a company or product is especially strong. These segments are typically too small to interest companies with large market shares, but they are profitable and unlikely to attract competitors.

Nomenclature System

A nomenclature system is a structure for establishing a blueprint for name development. These systems now encompass the brand's tone of voice and parameters for language use to ensure differentiation and consistency.

Nometrics

An Interbrand proprietary research tool providing decision support for potential brand name and tagline candidates. Each potential brand name is evaluated using specific criteria, including pronunciation, imagery and personality associations, name acceptability as well as "fit" with brand concept and more. There are both quantifiable and qualitative aspects within Nometrics.

Offer

There are two general definitions of offer: first, the terms and conditions under which a product or service is presented for sale (price, quantity, delivery date, shipping costs, guarantee, and so on). And second, the design, features, quality, packaging, and distribution (together with associated services such as financing, warranties, and installation) of the product or service a company *offers* for sale.

One-to-one Marketing

Often called *personalized marketing*, this is when a company tries to make a unique product offering to each potential buyer. It is most practical on the internet because a website can track a customer's preferences and offer buying suggestions. For example, Amazon tracks individual customer histories and inclinations and makes specific, customized product suggestions.

Opportunity Model

An opportunity model collects and studies past and present information in order to identify trends, forces, and conditions to help management choose appropriate strategies to meet company goals. The Interbrand Brand Opportunity Model employs a construct of differentiation, credibility, relevance, and stretch to determine the unique positioning for a brand.

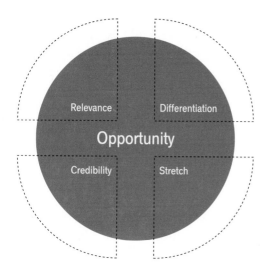

Organic Growth

This is the rate of business growth that results from increasing production and sales and reinvesting revenue back into the company, rather than growth that comes as a result of mergers, acquisitions, and takeovers.

Brand Fact:
Centrally managed brands, with consistent execution globally, are the preferred means of brand management by 60 percent of executives. Yet 67 percent agree or strongly agree that local customization of a brand has a positive impact on sales, according to the Economist Intelligence Unit.

"You can't build a reputation on what you're going to do."

Henry Ford

Brand Fact:
Most major marketers allocate between 4 and 10 percent of their measured media spending to the online channel, according to Booz Allen Hamilton.

Notes:

....
....
....
....
....
....
....
....
....
....
....
....
....
....
....
....
....
....
....

Packaged Goods

These are products that are packaged by their manufacturer; they typically carry a low unit price, are distributed through food and drug stores, are heavily promoted (usually in mass media), and are bought and consumed frequently (toothpaste, for example).

Packaging

Generally speaking, packaging is all the activities and materials associated with designing and producing a product's container or wrapper for presentation to the public. In addition to protecting products, packaging provides important information and helps promote whatever's inside.

Packaging Design

Packaging design can be viewed in four different ways: as a means of protecting whatever is inside the container; as a contributor to how much the product costs; as the blank slate on which to promote a product's attributes and benefits; and as part of the product experience. Packaging design has evolved way beyond simple functional benefits and is now a sophisticated and powerful example of designers' capabilities. A package design is on-shelf for approximately five years, so the design must meet a great deal of criteria to be successful.

Parent Brand

The parent is the main brand in a brand family. It is the master, primary brand and it takes on an endorsing function for one or more sub-brands.

Parity

Parity is when a company's products or performance are no better and no worse than the competition's. It is also when consumers see no real difference between brands in the same category. With gasoline, for example, consumers see no real difference other than price. Brand is a means to overcome parity from commodities to luxury items.

Passing Off

The name given to a legal action brought to protect the "reputation" of a particular trademark/brand/get-up. In essence, the action is designed to prevent others from trading on the reputation/goodwill of an existing trademark/brand/get-up. The action is only available in those countries that recognize unregistered trademark rights (for example the UK and US). In some countries, it is called *unfair competition action*.

Penetration

Penetration is often short for market penetration, and refers to the extent that individuals or organizations in a particular market have already purchased a brand, and/or the degree to which a product or service is known among potential buyers. This is a growth strategy in which a company concentrates efforts in its target market in order to increase market share or enhance its competitive advantage. Market share increase can be accomplished by attracting buyers of competitive brands; persuading current customers to buy more; offering an improved or revised product; and/or by attracting consumers who don't currently buy in the product category.

Perception

Perception is the way individuals interpret the stimuli around them. It's an impression of reality based on beliefs, needs, attitudes, events, and people and it influences actions and behaviors. In a branding context, perceptions can and do affect buying decisions.

Personality

Personality is attributing human characteristics (particularly emotional or attitudinal) to a brand. For example, Coke is fun, McDonald's is happy, Volvos are safe, and so on. Investing brands with personality is achieved through advertising, promotion, packaging, and/or corporate graphics, but also increasingly through the qualities of the people who work for the brand. Furthermore, personality should be created to reflect or complement the brand's target customers, and understanding their characteristics aids this. Personality is a critical component of brand building because product parity exists in most markets, so differentiation and choice may largely be the result of what a customer "likes" emotionally.

Brand Fact:
According to Datamonitor,
4.4 percent of lower income
consumers do not consider brand as
an important factor in their
purchasing criteria.

Notes:

Perceptual Mapping

This is a process used in marketing research to understand what selected customers think about current and future products; how they perceive different companies, products, or brand attributes; and how they would rank whatever is being researched versus its competition. One of the tools used in the process is a perception-mapping graphic that visualizes where customers place a product or supplier in relation to other products and suppliers. (Also called *position mapping*.)

Permission Marketing

This is a type of marketing that offers consumers the opportunity to receive marketing information (newsletters, for example), new product release information, or announcements of upcoming events. Author Seth Godin, in his book *Permission Marketing*, made up the term. Permission marketing allows marketers to communicate messages relevant to their brand, and to develop an ongoing positive relationship with consumers.

Personality

See page 95

Point of Purchase (POP)

These are promotional materials placed at the contact sales point in a retail store to attract consumer interest or call attention to a special offer. Point of purchase displays are usually placed near check-out counters, and are packages, signs, display cartons, and so on, designed to provide additional product information and to motivate impulse buying.

Point of Sale (POS)

This is a term for materials that are designed to increase sales and introduce products (like outside signs, window displays, counter pieces, display racks, and self-service cartons). However, it can also refer to a data collection system that electronically receives and stores bar code information from sales transactions.

Portfolio

This refers to the sum of the brand's architecture or all the brand holdings under control of ownership. The portfolio is managed individually and holistically in an attempt to derive benefits of association and individuality.

Portfolio Analysis

This is a strategic planning tool that helps determine marketing strategy. It evaluates a product's growth rate and relative market share, and compares it with the other products and services in a portfolio. The outcome objective is to see which products are performing well and should be continued, and which are underperforming and should be discontinued.

Portfolio Management

This is the business process (based on a portfolio analysis) whereby a business unit decides on its mix of products and services, the staffing that's needed, and how the marketing budget should be allocated. In a branding context, it is the practice of managing across and within all the brands in an owner's portfolio.

Positioning

The distinctive position that a brand adopts in its competitive environment to ensure that individuals in its target market can distinguish the brand from others. Positioning involves the careful manipulation of every element of the marketing mix. Positioning defines to whom the brand is trying to appeal, what the basis of that appeal is going to be, and why key targets should believe the message.

Positioning Statement

The positioning statement is the articulation of the positioning strategy. It can be an inspirational, persuasive, or powerful set of words or

P

images that creates a common understanding and aligns beliefs and actions. It becomes the platform for all brand communications.

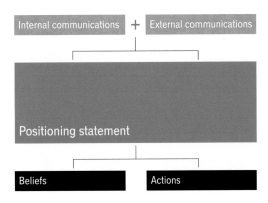

Power Branding

A strategy in which every product in a company's range has its own brand name which functions independently, unsupported by either the company's corporate brand or its other product brands. Power branding is a resource-intensive strategy, since each brand must be commercially promoted and legally protected. The strategy is used mainly by manufacturers of consumer goods. Lever's and Procter & Gamble's detergents are good examples of power brands.

Preference

A basic objective of advertising and promotion campaigns is preference, establishing that one brand is more desirable than its competition. Brand preference is necessary for a consumer to buy a product (just as brand loyalty is necessary for repeat purchases).

Premium

In branding, this refers to the price differential a brand owner receives over like offers. A strong brand can deliver extra revenue based on the perceptions of its quality, uniqueness, and other associations.

Prescreen

Prescreening helps reduce the risk of wasting time and money evaluating names that are clearly unavailable for use. Names are screened for identical and confusingly similar marks (including exact hits, near identicals, and phonetic variations) in the appropriate trademark class(es) for pertinent goods/services. Key considerations take into account whether or not a particular mark is descriptive, or if the mark is in what can be considered a crowded field. Results of the prescreen help determine whether or not a name is a candidate for the next level of screening — the full legal search.

Primary and Secondary Colors

The primary colors of a brand refer to the colors the corporate brand will always appear in, for example, the red and yellow of McDonald's. The secondary colors are chosen to complement the primary colors and add variety and depth to an identity.

Private Label Brands

Private label brands (or services) are usually provided by one company and sold under another company's name. They are most often lower cost alternatives to regional, national, or international brands. Since private label branding is most usually done by retailers, wholesalers, or dealers, the result is often called a *store brand*. In recent years, large retail and wholesale organizations like Kmart, Sears, and Kroger have begun to advertise their private brands extensively, and market them nationally and internationally.

Product

A product is a combination of functional, psychological, and need-satisfying features that a seller offers to a buyer. These features can include goods, services, ideas, places, and organizations. A product is physical and tangible, while a service isn't.

Brand Fact:
The Economist Intelligence Unit found 67 percent of 145 executives said their companies had revised or updated their brand. 21 percent of them had engaged a brand consultancy.

Notes:

....

....

....

....

....

....

....

....

....

....

....

....

....

....

....

....

....

....

....

....

Product Differentiation

This is a strategy that uses design innovations, packaging, advertising, and positioning to make a clear distinction between products serving the same market segment. Basically, it is the development of unique product differences with the intent to influence demand. The differences, however, can sometimes be very minor, like a simple change in packaging or a new advertising theme.

Product Life Cycle

Product life cycle is a concept that says there is a similarity between the life span of a product and that of a human. It suggests that products go through four stages from birth to death: introductory (slow sales growth that follows a new product introduction); growth (rapid sales growth as a product is accepted); maturity (the leveling off of sales when a product has been accepted by most potential buyers); and decline (the weakening of sales as a product is replaced or falls into disfavor). This idea is used to formulate marketing strategies for each of the four stages, but there is a difference of opinion about whether products go through this cycle in any predictable way or not.

Product/Market Expansion Matrix

This construct from Igor Ansoff, a leading figure in strategic management, claims that businesses should focus their strategic thinking on three key elements: defining their core objectives; whether they should diversify for growth and, if so, into what areas; and how they should leverage their current position. Lauded for its simplicity, the matrix is also disparaged for the assumption that growth opportunities always exist.

Product Placement

This is a form of advertising and promotion in which characters in a play, film, television series, music video, video game, or book use an actual commercial product. In the last few years, product placement has become rather a large business, with producers enjoying often large amounts of additional revenue to have their hero drive a specific car or drink a specific cola.

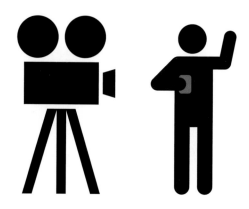

Product Proliferation

This is a charge sometimes leveled against companies for marketing so many new products that economic resources are wasted. The consumer becomes confused, and mistakes are made in product purchase. (Think about how many toothpaste choices are currently available – whitening or not, containing mouthwash or not, tartar control or not, and so on.)

Proof Points

Areas in which the customer has exposure and/or interaction with the brand. Sometimes referred to as *moments of truth*, these are opportunities to achieve loyalty or turn the customer off. Procter & Gamble speaks of its two moments of truth – when a customer purchases a product and when they actually use it.

Promiscuity

This is when consumers exhibit an absence of brand loyalty, when they change their support of one brand for a competitor. It is also called *brand switching* and it's the opposite of brand loyalty (see Loyalty). Often an issue in commodity situations, promiscuity signals the brand owner that the unique value proposition is virtually non-existent.

P

> ## Our business model doesn't rely on hit products – it relies on the power of our brands."
>
> Bob Eckert, Mattel

Notes:

Promise

A brand promise states the nature of the reciprocal relationship between the brand and its audience. It communicates the benefits and lifestyle enhancements a customer can expect and, like any contract between two parties, defines what each party can expect from the other. A brand must not overpromise or credibility is questioned and consumer disappointment will certainly result.

Promotion

Promotion is any technique that persuasively communicates favorable information about a seller's product to potential buyers through the broadest spectrum of communications media, including advertising, personal selling, sales promotion, public relations, and so on.

Prototype

A prototype is one of the early and important steps in new product development. It is a first working model (and in the case of a new service, it is a detailed plan and explanation). In both cases, a prototype is made specifically for testing because, for all intents and purposes, it is the actual product in appearance, characteristics, and performance.

Psychographic Segmentation

This divides markets into individual segments based on a psychographic analysis – a technique that investigates how people live, what interests them, and their likes and dislikes. It is also called a *lifestyle analysis* or AIO because it relies on a number of statements about a person's **a**ctivities, **i**nterests, and **o**pinions.

Public Relations

Simply stated, public relations is an activity intended to build relationships between any kind of organization and its key audiences. It communicates with chosen sectors of the public to influence their feelings, opinions, or beliefs about a person, product, company, or idea. PR is handled either by an in-house department, or in conjunction with a public relations firm – an organization that develops and implements programs to manage publicity, image, and public perceptions.

Publicity

Publicity is newsworthy information about a person, group, event, or product distributed through the communications media and intended to attract public notice. It is a form of promotion that makes something known, spreads information, and attracts support. And, unlike advertising, since the information has some measure of news value, it is free. (Obviously, costs would be incurred if an agency or consultant were under contract to serve this function.)

Pure Competition

This is a marketing situation in which a large number of competitive products can't be differentiated from each other. Since no single brand can significantly influence pricing, the door is open for additional competitors who might try to grab market share.

Pyramid

The brand pyramid was developed by author and professor Leslie de Chernatony and is comprised of attributes, benefits, emotional rewards, values, and personality traits. It is meant to match the buyer's behavior to the brand in order to instill and maintain loyalty. Often compared to Maslow's hierarchy of needs, but in the context of branding and brand decision-making.

Notes:

Qualitative Research

Qualitative research focuses on subjective data that is not easily translated into numbers. It is a method of gathering information on consumer preferences, beliefs, and emotions, and it does so through group interaction and discussion. It investigates perceptions, opinions, brand images, brand personality, and testing of advertisements, and it seeks insights into marketing situations that don't require statistical accuracy.

Quantitative Research

Quantitative research is based on objective data that is collected, can be subjected to statistical analysis, and can be expressed numerically. It is consumer research, often surveys, that is conducted with a large enough sample to produce statistically reliable information that's often used to project outcomes. It is used to determine performance ratings, the importance of different customer needs, current products and customer satisfaction levels, probability of repurchase, and product preferences.

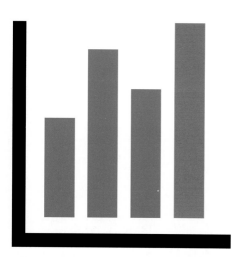

Range Branding

Range branding is extending a single brand across several related categories. Harley-Davidson, for example, markets motorcycles, tee shirts, leather jackets, coffee cups, and so on. There is less risk involved in range branding than stretching the original brand to entirely new categories.

Reach

This is the percentage of consumers in a target market exposed at least once to a particular advertisement in a particular period of time. TV commercials typically have very high reach. (Although cable TV programs have a much more limited reach, they are more focused and can be more effectively targeted.) Reach figures have no meaning without an associated time period. For example, an illustration of a valid reach figure would be "XYZ commercial had a one-day reach of 1,565 per million on October 14, 2006."

Rebrand

This is when a company updates or revises a brand based on internal or external pressures. It is often necessary after a merger, or if a brand has outgrown its identity in the marketplace. Rebranding can involve radical changes to a brand's logo, name, image, marketing strategy, or advertising approach, or the changes can be superficial. Rebranding can be applied to new products, mature products, or even unfinished products. A rebrand for the sake of rebranding offers great risk. Any rebranding should have a business situation as the catalyst.

"The essence of a strategy is not the structure of a company's products and markets, but the dynamics of its behavior."

George Stalk

Brand Fact:

In his book, *Profit from the Core*, Chris Zook states that 47 percent of new product launches fail after the first three years in market.

Notes:

Recall

Recall refers to a customer being able to remember a specific brand when given a category of products without any mention of the brands in it. This is also called *unaided recall*. On the other hand, *aided recall* (also called *brand recognition*) measures the extent to which a brand is remembered when its name is prompted. For example, "Are you familiar with the Sony brand?" Companies are interested in high levels of unaided recall because the first brand mentioned has a distinct competitive advantage over the competition. See Top of Mind

Recognition See Brand Awareness

Refresh See Revitalization

Relationship Marketing

This refers to marketing with the expectation of a long-term relationship rather than a one-shot transaction. This removes the need for an individual transaction having to be profitable, because the focus is on the relationship being profitable over its lifetime. This approach is able to work because marketers can now segment their target markets all the way down to individuals, and are able to understand the value each one brings to a relationship over time.

Relative Market Share

This is the size of one company's share versus its competitors. Having a large share allows for economies of scale in product development, manufacturing, and marketing. It also puts a company or brand in a stronger position in customers' minds, and this has a positive impact all along the marketing and selling process.

Relaunch

This is a strategy that focuses on finding new markets, untapped market segments, new product uses, and/or ways to stimulate increased use of a product by existing customers. A relaunched product has usually been changed in some basic way so it can be promoted as "new and improved."

Relevance

See page 105

Repositioning

Repositioning means changing the position of a product or service in the minds of customers, either because the original was a failure, or because of changes in the marketplace, or to allow for a new product introduction. Some potentially valuable products don't meet sales objectives because they were inadequately launched or positioned ineffectively, and it is almost always possible to enhance their value by repositioning them.

Reputation

This is the overall impression made by a company or brand based on belief systems, values, and practices.

Response Rate

The percentage of responses received from a direct marketing campaign (typically a mailing). It is also known as *completion rate* or *return rate* and is the overall number of people who responded divided by the total number of mailings, expressed as a percentage. For example, if 100 surveys are sent and 25 are completed and returned, the return rate is 25 percent.

Retail Audit

A retail audit is the systematic evaluation of a company's total retailing effort (although it can concentrate on one specific aspect of it). A company conducts a retail audit to study what it's doing, to evaluate how it's performing, and to make decisions about future actions.

Relevance

Relevance is the appropriateness or "fit" of a brand with the functional and emotional needs of its target market. Ultimately, customers determine relevance; that is, a brand is only relevant if customers perceive it to be. The history of business is strewn with brands their owners thought would be relevant but consumers decided weren't, like the Edsel.

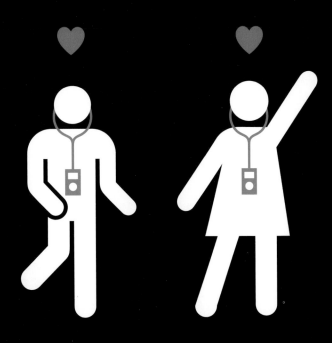

"There is a very fine line between good customer service and stalking."

Tara Lemmey

Retailing

Retailing is selling products and services to consumers for their personal or family use. (In this sense, service providers like dentists, hotels, hair salons, and online stores like amazon.com are also retailers.) By contrast, *wholesale* is selling goods and services for resale.

Many businesses, like Home Depot, are both retailers and wholesalers because they sell to consumers and also to building contractors. Other businesses, like The Limited, are both retailers and manufacturers. Regardless of their other functions, these businesses are still considered retailers when they interact with the final user of their product or service.

Retention

Retention can be used in two business senses: the percentage of customers who return on a regular basis to do business with a company or brand, and in a sense similar to *recall*, a consumer's ability remember a specific brand.

Return on (Brand) Investment

This is a method companies use to calculate a brand's financial value compared with the amount of money being spent on it. The brand's profitability, or lack of profitability, is expressed as a percentage. Further, these analytics provide prescriptive information on which to base sound business decisions for future investment in the brand.

Notes:

Revitalization

Revitalization is energizing a once-popular brand that has lost its appeal due to changes in the marketing environment, competitors' strategies, consumer behavior, and so on. It's a process undertaken either by the company that originally launched the brand, or by a different company that has acquired it. Repackaging and repositioning are usually necessary steps if success is to be achieved, and are often a less costly strategy than creating a new brand. Revitalizing a brand can provide a company with a significant advantage in a mature market.

Role of Brand

An aspect of Interbrand's brand valuation methodology, this is the assessment of the proportion of intangible earnings that can be attributed to the brand in each market segment. This is calculated by first identifying the various drivers of demand for the branded business, then determining the degree to which each driver is directly influenced by the brand.

Rollout

Similar to a soft launch, a brand rollout employs a measured step-by-step timetable to communicate with one audience after another, often in different geographic or demographic segments.

Brand Fact:
The Economist Intelligence
Unit found that 81 percent
of senior executives believe
their corporate brand is critical,
very important, or important as
an asset of the business.
79 percent said their products'
brands were critical, very
important, or important.

"All the great things are simple, and many can be expressed in a single word: Freedom. Justice. Honor. Duty. Mercy. Hope."

Winston Churchill

Brand Fact:

Red Stripe beer sales increased by 50 percent after Tom Cruise was shown drinking it in the film *The Firm*, according to Datamonitor.

Notes:

....

....

....

....

....

....

....

....

....

....

....

....

....

....

....

....

....

....

Sales

The confirmation of a commercial exchange. In retail, a sale refers to products offered at less than the original price to increase store traffic and attract new customers. Sales can be done in person or over the phone, through email or via mail. The sales process generally includes: assessing customer needs; presenting product features and benefits that address those needs; and negotiation on price, delivery, and other considerations. The primary function of professional sales is to turn prospective customers into actual customers by generating and closing leads, educating prospects, and satisfying needs.

Salience

Salience is defined both as top-of-mind brand awareness and as overall brand prominence based on various performance measures. Salience explains why certain brands perform better than others even though there may only be minor tangible differences between them.

Sampling

Sampling is based on the idea that a small number of randomly chosen people from a target audience will tend to have the same characteristics, in the same proportion, as the total population of that audience. After a sample is determined (typically by a market research firm), a survey is distributed that is designed to poll those selected about whatever subject the survey was designed to investigate.

Segment

A segment is a group of buyers within a market who have relatively similar wants and needs.

Segmentation

This is a marketing strategy in which large, heterogeneous markets are broken down into small, more homogeneous segments, and then individual marketing programs are developed for each.

Segment–Target–Position Strategy

Segmentation means dividing a market into distinct groups of customers (segments) who behave in the same way or have similar needs. Each of these segments can then be targeted with specific marketing strategies such as:

- *Expansion*, in which one product is targeted to several segments, thus expanding its market
- *Concentrated*, in which a company targets one product to one segment
- *Product line*, in which new products in the same category are introduced into the segment, giving customers greater choice and the company protection from competition
- *Differentiated* in which a company operates in several or all segments at the same time and targets different products to each.

Self-image

This is when consumers buy certain brands primarily to make a statement about who they think they are and how they see their place in society. See Luxury Brands

Service Brand/Marketing

The service sector of the business world deals with marketing and selling intangible products instead of physical goods. Nail salons, travel agencies, insurance companies, lawyers, and so on are in the service sector, and what they sell requires branding and marketing just as tangible products do.

Seven P's

In addition to the widely recognized Four P's (product, pricing, promotion, place), more recent discussion has included three more variables known together as the *extended marketing mix*. These are:

- *People:* any person representing the brand and interacting with customers impacts the brand experience. As a result, these resources must be appropriately trained in the brand's attributes and values, be well motivated to

70/30 Rule

Applied more for context than numerical accuracy, 70/30 concerns the relative weighting given to the elements that must remain absolutely consistent in managing a brand versus the flexibility granted to its managers. Consistency is a key principle of branding, but a brand must be allowed to adjust appropriately to local markets; capitalize on new strategic directions; and evolve to keep a competitive edge. So, 70 percent consistency and 30 percent flexibility.

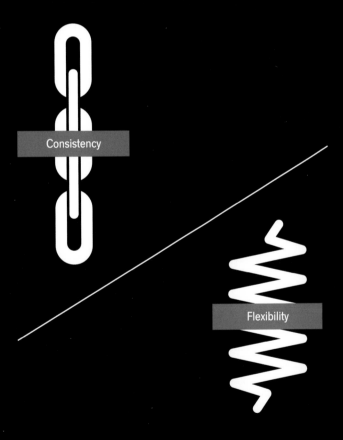

support and evolve the brand, and be an ambassador and representative of the brand.

- *Process:* these are the detailed situations where a customer can come in contact with the brand and that are critical to brand loyalty.
- *Physical evidence:* this readily exists in the realm of tangible products but in the case of services the brand cannot be truly experienced before it is delivered. Potential customers may perceive a greater risk when deciding whether or not to use a service. To mitigate this potential risk, customers must be allowed to test the service, be exposed to actual advocates, or be provided with a risk-free trial to help in the decision.

70/30 Rule

See page 111

Share of Mind

Although share of mind is the relative amount of attention a brand commands from its target audience, it is more complicated than, for example, the attention people pay to Pepsi versus Coke. Share of mind involves everything customers are thinking about, and what portion of that is devoted to an individual company, product, or service.

Share of Voice (SOV)

This is a brand's share of all the measured media in a predefined category. For example, if total tourism advertising in the US is $100 billion and an individual company spends $10 billion, they would have a 10 percent SOV.

Share of Wallet

Share of wallet is a percentage of how much consumers spend in total versus how much they spend on a specific brand. For example, if someone spends an average of $500/month on all their credit cards and spends $250/month on their Visa card – Visa would have a 50% share of wallet.

Notes:

Shelf Impact

Shelf impact is the ability of a brand, by virtue of its design, to stand apart from its competition on store shelves. With over 25,000 products in the average supermarket, the importance of shelf impact is clear.

Sonic Branding

Sonic branding is using a specific piece of music or a special sound to identify and advertise a product, service, or company. With enough repetitions, the sonic brand is very powerful and companies are beginning to use it everywhere current or future customers may be listening – radio and television, web-based communications, and even custom cell-phone rings. Interbrand's Brand Acoustics practice integrates sonic branding into overall branding programs as it reflects another touch point for brand awareness and differentiation.

Sponsorship

This is when a company subsidizes an event, offering funding to a group, association, sporting body, and so on, in return for a range of promotional opportunities. Sponsorship is a form of below-the-line advertising, which is advertising by means other than the five major mediums (the press, television, radio, movies, and outdoors). In addition to sponsorship, below-the-line advertising uses direct mail, merchandising, trade shows, exhibitions, sales literature and catalogues, and so on.

S

Brand Fact:
A 2004 survey of 370 marketers found that 70 percent of marketing departments had undergone a reorganization in the previous three years, reports Booz Allen Hamilton.

Notes:

....
....
....
....
....
....
....
....
....
....
....
....
....
....
....
....

Standalone or Freestanding Brands

These are brand names and identities used for single products or services that are unrelated to other products or services in a company's portfolio. They are supported and managed independently, and have their own logos, colors, and identity standards. Plus, in some cases, they can even have their own architecture of sub-brands, product brands, and service brands.

Strategic Planning

This is the process that determines a company's objectives, courses of action, resource allocation, and what results can be reasonably expected. By calling this plan *strategic*, it is expected to operate on a large scale and take in "the big picture" (as opposed to a *tactical* plan which would focus more on individual activities). A *SWOT analysis* (**s**trengths, **w**eaknesses, **o**pportunities, and **t**hreats) can be part of strategic planning as it evaluates a company in terms of its advantages and disadvantages versus competitors, the requirements of its customers, and market/economic conditions.

Stretch

Refers to the ability of a brand to stretch within its category and into adjacent or distant categories. Brand extensions that stretch within the same category (toothpaste) are prevalent. So too are brands that move into adjacent categories, like cleansers. Less common are brands that stretch across multiple categories, although Virgin has demonstrated that it can achieve success across a wide variety.

Style Guides

Style guides generally lay out a brand's communications standards in terms of colors, font types and sizes, graphic design, language (sometimes music), and so on. The guide assures that a brand will have visual consistency no matter where it is seen or used.

Sub-brand

This is a brand that builds on its association with a masterbrand. Even though it has its own name and visual identity, it is designed to leverage the history and equity of the master-brand and stretch into a new category, benefit, or target.

Substitutes

These are products that consumers view as alternatives for other products. Consumer motivation to try a substitute can be driven by cost, health, or environmental concerns, and/or by social trends. As examples: sugar versus artificial sweeteners, eyeglasses versus contact lenses, plastic containers versus glass, aspirin versus other types of pain relievers. Substitutes have an obvious effect on brand loyalty and become real threats when products of firms in other industries enter a market.

Switching Costs

This refers to the hidden costs a consumer faces when changing from one product to another. There can be non-monetary psycho-logical or social costs, researching and learning costs, or simply the effort needed to inform friends and relatives about a new telephone number. Or the costs can be monetary, like exit fees, equipment, installation, and start-up, and so on. Switching costs affect competition. Consumers won't even switch to a lower cost supplier if the totality of the switching costs outweigh the price differential. If this happens, consumers are said to be *locked-in* to a supplier. And if a company manages this lock-in, it can raise prices to a certain point without fear of losing customers because the effects of switching keep them where they are.

Symbol See Logo

"I see the proper response to change and challenge as increased creativity."

Gene DeWitt

Tagline/Slogan

This is a short, distinctive, and easily recognizable phrase that accompanies a brand, conveys its promise and, in a few memorable words, captures the theme of the ad or commercial in which it appears. Taglines aid recall, like Avis's "We try harder."

The secret to creativity is knowing how to hide your sources."

Albert Einstein

Tagline/Slogan

See page 116

Tangible Assets

Tangible assets are defined as having physical substance such as land, buildings, inventory, computing equipment, cash, and often accounts receivable (even though it can be argued that accounts receivable don't have a *physical* existence). Tangible assets such as machinery are depreciated according to their useful life and wear and tear in the business, but not all tangible assets can be depreciated — land, for example. Tangible assets have traditionally dominated the balance sheet. Intangible assets have recently become more important on the balance sheet due to changes in accounting regulations around the world. See Intangible Assets

Target Audience

A specified audience or demographic group to which a product or service is marketed. It is often defined by age, gender, and/or socio-economics but target audiences can be internal or external, geographic, or loyal/nonloyal, and so on.

Target Marketing

This is marketing to a specific group of consumers (segments) who have similar characteristics, who behave in the same way, or who have similar needs. Once these segments are identified, a company develops a *targeting strategy* that positions its product or service for maximum appeal. A targeting strategy includes the number of segments to target, which ones to target, how many products to offer, and which products to offer to which segments.

Thought Leadership

A brand that influences a market based on original and innovative ideas, even though it may not have a leadership position in market share (Apple Computers, for example).

Tone of Voice

The personality or attitude of a brand that's communicated through its verbal communications is called tone of voice. Another way to differentiate like design and sonic branding, tone of voice should reflect the unique features of the brand and help to define its personality through written and oral communications.

Notes:

....
....
....
....
....
....
....
....
....
....
....
....
....
....
....
....
....

Brand Fact:
The Association of National Advertisers and Booz Allen Hamilton found that 66 percent of senior marketers believe their greatest need is to develop capabilities in consumer insights and return on investment (ROI) analytics.

T

"When you are headed toward true innovation, you will find yourself in an uncomfortable or unfamiliar area."

Cris Goldsmith

Top of Mind

Top of mind is generally a reference to aware-ness. For example, if a consumer is asked in a marketing survey to name the first branding company that comes to mind and she or he says "Interbrand," then it can be said that Interbrand has top-of-mind awareness. Top of mind is alternatively called *unaided recall*, and companies are interested in it because the first brand remembered or mentioned has a distinct competitive advantage over the competition.

Touch Points

Everywhere people come into contact with a brand is called a "touch point." Touch points can be product use, advertising, packaging, in-store displays, casual conversation, and so on. Branding is a holistic experience and brand owners must anticipate all possible interactions a consumer can have with a brand.

Trade Names

These are corporate names in a particular business under which a company operates. (PepsiCo and Miller Brewing Co. are examples). Trade names can also function as trademarks. See Trademark

Trademark

A trademark is a formally registered and distinctive symbol; it is any name, word, phrase, logo, design, image (or a combination of two or more) used by businesses to distinguish their products or services from the competition. A trademark is proprietary and is usually registered with global and regional trademark offices. It provides legal protection for exclusive use by its owner.

Trademark Infringement

This is the unauthorized use of a registered trademark by someone other than its owner, or use of a symbol that is confusingly similar. Trademark infringement usually applies when products or services are identical or similar to those the registration covers. When the products or services aren't identical, infringe-ment will generally be decided by considering whether or not there is "likelihood of confusion" that consumers will believe the products or services originated from the trademark owner.

Trendsetter

Someone or something that breaks a traditional mold or routine and gains a following because of that action. iMac is an example of trend-setting in design as office supplies now come in the familiar colors and translucent packaging of an iMac.

Notes:

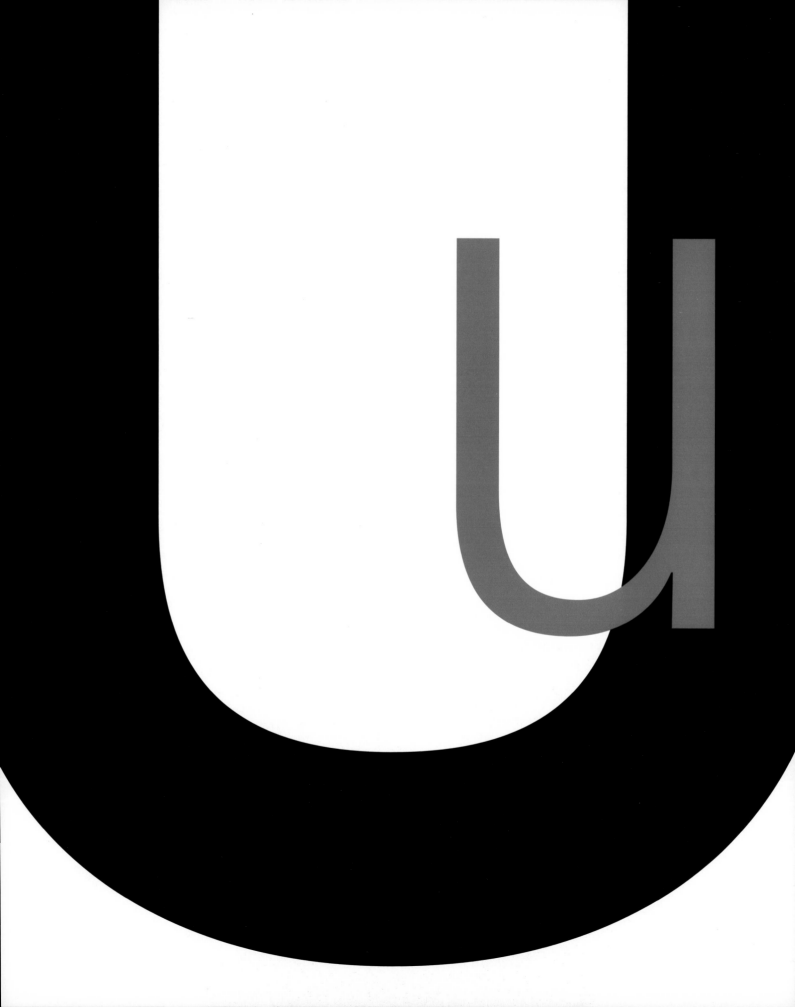

The power of intellectual capital is the ability to breed ideas that ignite value."

JPMorgan Chase 2001 Annual Report headline

Umbrella Brand

An umbrella brand is a parent brand that appears on a number of products that may each have separate identities. A strong umbrella brand can help a new product generate revenue because of quality and benefit associations. Individual branding, on the other hand, requires expensive advertising campaigns and extensive brand-building costs.

Unique Selling Proposition

A unique selling proposition (USP) is one of the fundamentals of effective marketing and advertising. It refers to a particular quality, feature, or benefit offered by a product or service that is important to customers and not available from the competition.

URL or Uniform Resource Locator

On the internet, this is the address of a web page on the World Wide Web. An URL (commonly pronounced "earl") includes a protocol prefix (http://, ftp://), a domain name (interbrand.com, brandchannel.com), and possibly a path and filename. The path and the filename are an opportunity to direct viewers beyond the normal "home" page of a website. In http://www.interbrand.com, http:// refers to the internet, Interbrand is the name of the company, and the .com shows it's a company. An URL is unique; no two can be alike.

User Segmentation

This is the process of grouping consumers into market segments based on what they desire from a product. For example, the toothpaste market may include one segment seeking cosmetic benefits such as white teeth and another seeking health benefits such as decay prevention.

Value Driver

Generally defined as any variable that impacts the health and value of an enterprise. In the context of branding, this refers to the tangible and intangible components of a brand that represent differentiation and relevance to the target audiences.

Value Proposition

A (brand) value proposition is a short, clear, simple statement containing the main reasons for choosing one brand over another. It includes what the target market is for a particular product, what key benefits will be delivered, and how much will be charged. It provides the rationale (tangible and intangible) for choosing one brand over another.

Notes:

U-V

Brand Fact:

CMO magazine reported that 58 percent of chief marketing officers surveyed agree or strongly agree that the marketing function is changing and that their primary challenge is to define their place in the organization.

Notes:

Verbal Identity

This is the way a brand communicates in words its name, its advertising and taglines, its marketing communications, its website copy, and the descriptions on its packaging.

Viral Marketing

Viral marketing is spreading a brand's message person to person via word of mouth. It encourages people to pass along marketing messages to friends, colleagues, and/or family, thereby creating exponential growth in the message's reach. It is nicknamed "viral" because the exposure to a message mimics passing a virus from one person to another. Typical techniques include email messages, jokes, web addresses, funny film clips, and games that get forwarded electronically by recipients.

Visibility

A desired result from brand investment is to gain greater visibility and awareness. This is the first step in communicating with desired audiences to try the brand and gain first-hand experience of its tangible and intangible benefits. Visibility has often been tied to traditional advertising but now has wider meaning in brands being used visibly by category influencers, such as personalities and characters in television and film.

Visual Identity

This is extending a company's brand in every possible way with every element contributing to a distinctive visual style. This includes where and how a logo is used, colors, type fonts and sizes, and imagery. The purpose of a company's visual identity is to set it apart from its competition and, in order to be effective and memorable, it has to be consistent across all media. See Brand Guidelines

Visual Language Concepts

A number of alternative visual strategies used to articulate different but related elements of the brand. Each concept will reflect the brand positioning and create a story using visuals rather than words.

Brand Fact:
The IDC CMO Advisory study found that the top three marketing measurement mandates from the CEO are:

1. Consistent metrics for ROI of marketing
2. Measurement of brand awareness and reputation
3. Consistent lead-generation metrics.

"All progress is based upon a universal, innate desire on the part of every organism to live beyond its income."

Samuel Butler

Wear Out

The point reached when a communications campaign loses effectiveness, due either to repeated overplay or the audience's wants and needs no longer being met by what is promised in the communication.

Notes:

....
....
....
....
....
....
....
....
....
....
....
....
....
....
....
....
....
....
....

Website

A website is a collection of linked, interconnected pages on the internet used to provide information about a company, organization, cause, or person. Websites can be purely informational, can serve marketing and advertising functions, and/or can be a point of interaction or sales. Another touch point in the brand experience, a website is an opportunity to communicate all that makes the brand unique.

Word of Mouth See Buzz

Wordmark

A wordmark is the way you write a name that is unique and ownable. It also refers to a logotype. It typically incorporates one or more unique characteristics such as a custom designed font, symbol, or graphic device.

Brand Fact:
Spencer Stuart's annual study shows that the average tenure of a chief marketing officer is a sobering 23.2 months, down from 23.6 months in 2004, and 23.5 months in 2005.

(Brand) Yield

This is a proprietary process, derived from Interbrand's Brand Valuation and Brand Equity Insights methodologies, which allows the modeling of an optimal portfolio of branding activities within a given budget, industry, and competitive environment.

Bibliography

Internet

Amos WEB GLOSS-Arama
http://www.amosweb.com/cgi-bin/awb_nav.pl?s=
gls&c=ind&a=a
(February 13, 2006)

Bloomberg Financial Glossary
http://www.bloomberg.com/analysis/glossary/bfglosa.htm
(February 19, 2006)

Brand Careers – Glossary
http://www.brandchannel.com/education_glossary.asp
(February 5, 2006)

Brand Glossary
http://www.venturerepublic.com/resources/brand_glossary.asp
(February 2, 2006)

Campbell R. Harvey, Hypertextual Finance Glossary
http://www.duke.edu/~charvey/Classes/wpg/glossary.htm
(February 23, 2006)

Chartered Institute of Marketing, The, Marketing Glossary
http://www.cim.co.uk/cim/ser/html/infQuiGlo.cfm?letter=A
(February 4, 2006)

CMO Lingo Lab Marketing Glossary
http://www.cmomagazine.com/glossary/
(February 6, 2006)

Dictionary of Marketing Terms
http://www.marketingpower.com/mg-dictionary.php?
(February 2, 2006)

Glossary
http://users.wbs.warwick.ac.uk/dibb_simkin/student/
glossary/index.html
(February 6, 2005)

Glossary
http://www.allaboutbranding.com/index.lasso?page=11,54,0
(February 7, 2006)

Glossary of Design Terms
http://edweb.sdsu.edu/courses/ET650_online/MAPPS/
Glossary.html
(February 12, 2006)

Glossary of Interactive Advertising Terms
http://www.adglossary.com/
(February 23, 2006)

Glossary of Marketing Definitions
http://www.ifla.org/VII/s34/pubs/glossary.htm
(February 7, 2006)

Glossary of Marketing Terms
http://www.marketing.org.au/glossary_of_marketing_terms.aspx
(March 8, 2006)

Hackers, Hits and Chats: An E-Commerce and Marketing
Dictionary of Terms
http://www.udel.edu/alex/dictionary.html
(February 5, 2006)

Market Research Terms and Methodologies
http://www.asiamarketresearch.com/glossary/
(February 5, 2006)

Marketing Dictionary, The
http://www.buseco.monash.edu.au/depts/mkt/dictionary/
(February 3, 2006)

Marketing Glossary
http://www.onpoint-marketing.com/marketing-glossary.htm
(February 9, 2006)

Marketing Terms and Definitions
http://marketing.about.com/cs/glossaryofterms/l/blglossary.htm
(February 8, 2006)

Money 101 Glossary
http://money.cnn.com/services/glossary/a.html
(February 15, 2006)

New York Times Glossary of Financial and Business Terms
http://www.nytimes.com/library/financial/glossary/
bfglosa.htm?oref=slogin
(February 3, 2006)

Online (Retail) Glossary
http://www.prenhall.com/rm_student/html/glossary/
a_gloss.html
(February 22, 2006)

Product Development and Management Association.
Glossary for New Product Development
http://www.pdma.org/library/glossary.html
(February 5, 2006)

"Good tactics can save even the worst strategy. Bad tactics will destroy even the best strategy."

General George S. Patton, Jr.

Quirk's Glossary
http://www.quirks.com/resources/glossary.asp
(February 5, 2006)

Scarcliff/Salvador Inc., Lexicon of Naming and Branding
http://www.scarcliff.com/naming_and_branding_lexicon.html#A
(February 4, 2006)

Texas Advertising, the University of Texas at Austin
http://advertising.utexas.edu/research/terms/

Trautmann, Carl O., Dictionary of Small Business
http://www.small-business-dictionary.org/default.asp?action=
A & term=showCart
(February 5, 2005)

Books

Baker, Michael John, ed. *Macmillan Dictionary of Marketing and Advertising*. London and New York: Palgrave Macmillan, 1998.

Bannock, Graham. *Dictionary of Business*. Princeton, NJ: Bloomberg Press, 2003.

Bennett, Peter D. *Dictionary of Marketing Terms*. Lincolnwood, Ill: NTC Business Books, 1995.

Carruth, Donald L. and Steven Austin Stovall. *NTC's American Business Terms Directory*. Lincolnwood, Ill: National Textbook Company, 1994.

Clemente, Mark M. *The Marketing Glossary*. New York: American Management Association, 1992.

Folsom, Davis W. *Understanding American Business Jargon*. Westport, Connecticut: Greenwood Press, 1997.

Friedman, Jack P. *Dictionary of Business Terms*. Hauppauge, NY: Barron's Educational Series, 2000.

Godin, Seth. *Permission Marketing: Turning Strangers into Friends and Friends into Customers*. New York: Simon & Schuster, 1999.

Govoni, Norman A. *Dictionary of Marketing Communications*. Thousand Oaks, CA: Sage Publications, 2004.

Hart, Norman A. *The CIM Marketing Dictionary*. London: Butterworth-Heinemann, 1996.

Imber, Jane and Betsey-Ann Toffler. *Dictionary of Marketing Terms*. Hauppauge, NY: Barron's Educational Series, 2000.

Isaacs, Alan and Elizabeth Martin. *The Oxford Dictionary for the Business World*. New York: Oxford University Press, 1993.

Koschnick, Wolfgang. *Dictionary of Marketing*. Brookfield, VT: Gower, 1995.

Lewis, Barbara R. and Dale Littler, eds. *The Blackwell Encyclopedia Dictionary of Marketing*. Cambridge, MA: Blackwell Publishers, 1997.

Mercer, David Steuart. *Marketing: the Encyclopedia Dictionary*. Malden, MA: Blackwell Publishers, 1999.

Neumeier, Marty, ed. *The Dictionary of Brand*. New York: AIGA, 2004.

Pallister, John and Alan Isaacs, *A Dictionary of Business*. New York: Oxford University Press, 2004.

Rosenberg, Jerry Martin. *Dictionary of Marketing and Advertising*. New York: J. Wiley, 1995.

Statt, David A. *The Routledge Dictionary of Business Management*. New York: Routledge, 2004.

Sutherland, Jonathan and Diane Canwell. *Key Concepts in Marketing*. London and New York: Palgrave Macmillan, 2004.

Tarcy, Brian. *The Business Words You Should Know*. Holbrook, MA: Adams Media Corp, 1997.

The Ultimate Business Dictionary; Defining the World of Work. Cambridge, MA: Perseus Publications, 2003.

Wendel, Charles B. *Business Buzzwords: Everything You Need to Know to Speak the Lingo of the 90's*. New York: Amacon, 1995.

Wilbur, Cross. *Prentice Hall Encyclopedia of Business Terms*. Englewood Cliffs, NJ: Prentice Hall, 2005.

Yadin, Daniel L. *The International Dictionary of Marketing*. London: Kogan Page, 2002.

Zook, Chris. *Profit from the Core*. Boston, MA: Harvard Business School Press, 2001.

Brand Fact:

SelfServiceWorld magazine found that 55 percent of US online consumers have researched a product online and then purchased that same product offline. This equates to more than 40 million consumers – an 8 percent increase over 2004.

 © Interbrand 2007

All rights reserved. No reproduction, copy or transmission of this publication may be made without written permission.

No paragraph of this publication may be reproduced, copied or transmitted save with written permission or in accordance with the provisions of the Copyright, Designs and Patents Act 1988, or under the terms of any licence permitting limited copying issued by the Copyright Licensing Agency, 90 Tottenham Court Road, London W1T 4LP.

Any person who does any unauthorised act in relation to this publication may be liable to criminal prosecution and civil claims for damages.

The author has asserted his right to be identified as the author of this work in accordance with the Copyright, Designs and Patents Act 1988.

First published 2007 by PALGRAVE MACMILLAN Houndmills, Basingstoke, Hampshire RG21 6XS and 175 Fifth Avenue, New York, N.Y. 10010 Companies and representatives throughout the world

PALGRAVE MACMILLAN is the global academic imprint of the Palgrave Macmillan division of St. Martin's Press, LLC and of Palgrave Macmillan Ltd. Macmillan® is a registered trademark in the United States, United Kingdom and other countries. Palgrave is a registered trademark in the European Union and other countries.

ISBN-13: 978–1–4039–9809–5
ISBN 10: 1–4039–9809–4

This book is printed on paper suitable for recycling and made from fully managed and sustained forest sources.

A catalogue record for this book is available from the British Library.

A catalog record for this book is available from the Library of Congress.

10 9 8 7 6 5 4 3 2 1
16 15 14 13 12 11 10 09 08 07

Printed and bound in Great Britain by Hobbs the Printers Ltd, Totton, Hants